PRAISE FOR WORK FROM THE I[

D1536302

"We all want to do w   g, and
meaningful—and Tammy Gooler Loeb shows us how. In *Work
from the Inside Out*, Tammy draws upon her twenty-plus years as
a career and executive coach to dispel the typical obstacles
that hold people back from pursuing more fulfilling work.
Here's to enjoying Monday mornings again!"

**—Dorie Clark, author of *Reinventing You* and
executive education faculty, Duke University
Fuqua School of Business**

"If you're contemplating a career switch, *Work from the Inside
Out* should be at the top of your booklist. With so many
options and obstacles, it's easy to second guess yourself and
become lost in the process. Tammy Gooler Loeb shows how
this is a normal (and helpful!) part of career exploration and
transition, and how to not allow fear and uncertainty to derail
your progress. Filled with relatable, inspiring stories and reflection questions that help you identify and conquer potential
hurdles, this book is a must-have companion to anyone
thinking about the next step in their career."

**—Dawn Graham, PhD, author of
*Switchers: How Smart Professionals
Change Careers and Seize Success***

"I really enjoyed reading *Work from the Inside Out*. It's an interesting read with captivating personal stories to inspire and motivate along with useful questions and activities to apply Tammy's insights directly to your life and career."

—Andy Molinsky, PhD, author of
Global Dexterity and Reach

"Many of us feel stuck in our careers at some point. We wonder, did we make the right choice? Should we pursue an alternate course? If so, how? Fortunately, Tammy Gooler Loeb provides some real-world solutions in her book, *Work from the Inside Out: Break Through Nine Common Obstacles and Design a Career that Fulfills You*. Combining insights from her podcast guests' experiences, and her own coaching practice, Gooler Loeb delivers answers that anyone thinking about a career move, or even career adjustment, will find valuable."

—John Baldoni, globally recognized executive coach, leadership educator, author of 15 books

"You're not too old, and it's not too late! If you are considering a career change, Tammy Gooler Loeb's *Work from the Inside Out* will not only give you confidence but a step-by-step actionable plan illustrated by stories of those who have walked the same path, to help you identify and land the career of your dreams."

—Laura Gassner Otting, author of *Limitless: How to Ignore Everybody, Carve Your Own Path, and Live Your Best Life*

"The time is perfectly right for a book like *Work from the Inside Out*. The world of work is going through seismic shifts and new horizons are appearing that many of us never thought possible. Through the stories of real, relatable people, and the questions their stories beg, Tammy Gooler Loeb helps us do something I can only describe as 'strategically feeling' our way through the question of our own careers and how we can find purpose, fulfillment, and joy in what we do every day—and make a living doing it. Buy it, read it, work it, and bring your work and life into alignment."

—Michael J. Leckie, consultant, speaker, and author of *The Heart of Transformation: Build the Human Capabilities That Change Organizations for Good*

"Tammy Gooler Loeb takes her depth of experience with clients and podcast guests to unpack the challenges of what is keeping us from fulfilling work and how to make a greater impact in the future."

—Diana Wu David, author of *Future Proof: Reinventing Work in an Age of Acceleration*

"No matter what your age or your responsibilities, it's never too late to change jobs or careers. The inspiring stories and practical advice in this excellent book by executive and career coach Tammy Gooler Loeb will give you the tools you need to get unstuck in the workplace and no longer dread going to work on Monday."

—Mac Prichard, Host, *Find Your Dream Job* podcast

"As a career and executive coach, Tammy Gooler Loeb has made it her mission to help others live their best lives. Well, in her terrific new book, *Work from the Inside Out*, Tammy does for her readers what she does for her clients—helping us to discover our passion and our purpose. Through story after story, gleaned from interactions with colleagues, clients, and podcast guests, we are both informed and inspired from start to finish. Like having a career coach in a book, reading *Work from the Inside Out* will help you to reflect on your own career journey...as you set out to write—or to rewrite—your own career success story."

—Todd Cherches, CEO of BigBlueGumball, and author of *VisuaLeadership: Leveraging the Power of Visual Thinking in Leadership and in Life*

"Careers are not formed in a straight line. Boy, ain't that the truth! Seems we don't recognize that reality until the straight line we'd envisioned takes a turn. Sometimes a crooked twist. Through insightful stories and guidance, Tammy shows how these twists and turns can lead to something better. *Work from the Inside Out* serves as a guide, helping you find and embrace the opportunities to be found on the windy path of your career."

—Jennifer J. Fondrevay, founder, Day1 Ready M&A Consultancy, bestselling author of *NOW WHAT? A Survivor's Guide for Thriving Through Mergers & Acquisitions*

"This book can change your life. Tammy Gooler Loeb draws on her savviness and years of experience working with clients to offer readers enlightening perspectives on the most common obstacles to significant career change. The book is full of riveting and inspiring stories that show that change at any age is possible."

—Ofer Sharone, PhD, author of *Flawed System/Flawed Self: Job Searching and Unemployment Experiences*

"I am a big believer in the power of story to inspire and to show us how to transform challenges into opportunities. In *Work from the Inside Out*, career and executive coach Tammy Gooler Loeb offers her readers all of that, as well as the resources to take the next steps in creating a more satisfying career. Anyone seeking to develop the confidence, clarity, and fortitude to move in a new direction needs this book."

—Gina Warner, Founder, Badass Women's Book Club

WORK FROM THE INSIDE OUT

WORK FROM THE INSIDE OUT

Break Through Nine Common Obstacles
and Design a Career That Fulfills You

Tammy Gooler Loeb

BAY WAY
PRESS

ISBN: 979-8-9854513-0-6 (paperback)
ISBN: 979-8-9854513-2-0 (hardcover)
ISBN: 979-8-9854513-1-3 (e-book)

Library of Congress Control Number: 2021925851

Edited by Jocelyn Carbonara
Proofread by Jacki Santoro
Cover design by Adam Renvoize
Interior design by Jenny Lisk
Author photograph by Kimberly Butler

Published by Bay Way Press, Newton, Massachusetts

To my parents, Ed and Gloria Gooler, who raised me to believe that careers are intended to be fulfilling pursuits. I am deeply grateful for your unending encouragement, and the inspiring example you set by doing meaningful work.

CONTENTS

Introduction   1

1. Fear: Friend or Foe?   13

2. It's Never Too Late   35

3. Too Many Responsibilities   51

4. Careers Are Not Formed in a Straight Line   69

5. Don't Default to What You're Good At   87

6. Success Is Not a Destination   107

7. You Need to Network, but Not Just for a Job   133

8. I'm Not Qualified. Do I Belong Here?   155

9. Uncertainty Is a Fact of Life   171

   Conclusion   203

   A Note from Tammy   211

   Resources   213

   What You Can Do Now   221

   Work with Tammy   223

   Notes   225

   Acknowledgments   229

   About the Author   231

INTRODUCTION

Your work is going to fill a large part of your life, and the only way to be truly satisfied is to do what you believe is great work. And the only way to do great work is to love what you do. If you haven't found it yet, keep looking. Don't settle. As with all matters of the heart, you'll know when you find it.

—STEVE JOBS

As a little girl in the 1960s, while other kids were all excited about Batman and Robin, I admired author and disability rights activist Helen Keller like a superhero. Helen lost her eyesight and hearing as a toddler. I was in awe of her tenacity to break through her communication challenges and the courage it took to function in a world that was limited in its capacity to engage with her.

When adults would ask me, "What do you want to be when you grow up?" I would say, "I want to be a teacher of the blind and deaf." At other times I would declare, "I'm going to be the first Jewish lady president!" While neither profession came to fruition, there was a foundation forming so deep within me that I could feel it in my bones. I was determined to *make a positive difference in people's lives,* and even then, I imagined that my efforts would ripple out beyond my immediate reach.

This vision has driven me ever since and remains at the core of every move I make in my career.

From that early age, I was already aiming to *work from the inside out.* Some might describe *working from the inside out* as having a calling, a passion, or working in alignment with one's values. When you work from the inside out, the focus is less on what job you are *doing* and more about who or how you are *being* when engaged in it. For example, whether I had become a teacher or the president, either would have qualified as *work from the inside out,* because my deeper sense of purpose would have been drivers of those jobs.

While this concept of *inside out* might seem abstract, it is connected to something we all possess: intuition. Many of us have wished we had listened to our inner thoughts and trusted our intuition about a problem or situation. Instead, we allowed our logical mind or the opinions of others to sway us toward a different course of action.

Prior to being a career and executive coach over the past two decades, I worked in several different fields earlier in my professional life. More than once I became deeply unhappy at work due to elements within each situation that did not align with my values or goals. And several times I remained in the job longer than I should have because I was either unclear about what I wanted to do next or I wasn't feeling energetic enough to engage in a job search. Sometimes I knew I was staying in the job too long, and other times I wasn't as clear that it was time to move on. In either case, I was not heeding what my inner voice was telling me.

When we tune in to listen to our "gut," that intuitive voice within, we make better choices and follow through on decisions in ways that suit us more authentically. We are more comfortable in our own skin. In his book, *Blink: The Power of Thinking Without Thinking,*[1] Malcolm Gladwell makes the case with research-based and anecdotal evidence that quick thoughts, snap judgments, and intuitive hunches help us make better decisions than longer, analytical thought processes. While there are uses for in-depth analyses, too often people do not trust their instincts, which leads to less effective decisions.

As children, we are educated through school and groomed by our families to become solid, productive members of society. By the middle of our high school years, we are pummeled with inquiries from well-intentioned adults: What are you interested in? What do you want to do? Where do you want to go to college? While this may not reflect your individual experience, most of us grew up assuming we would become adults with careers or jobs.

I recall having these conversations with my father and mother, and I feel fortunate in that they always encouraged me to identify career pathways that would be rewarding and meaningful. But for many, we envisioned those expectations evolving into an identity of what we were to become: lawyer, nurse, carpenter, engineer, or teacher—examples of professions that create an image of a well-formed, good life. Once we were established in our profession, our plan became to increase our level of responsibility and income while raising a family, all tied up into a neat, tidy package.

Then thirty-plus years later, we retire, put up our feet, and say, "OK, all done!"

Is that all there is to having a good life? Is that an *inside out* life? For some people, it could be, if they are delighted and engaged in their work. For many others, the stereotypical scenario just described would probably be an *outside in* life. Why? For one thing, most teenagers are not clear about their goals or aspirations, and often there is external pressure on them to choose a path and stick with it. With the high cost of education, many families steer their children toward majors or vocations they believe will enable them to "get a good job" once they graduate. That is definitely the *outside in* approach! While their intentions are positive, to help launch their kids into adulthood and the world of work, trying to squeeze a round peg into a square hole does not work in the long run. There is a better way—the *inside out* way—which is why I wrote this book.

As I stated earlier, I always wanted to make a positive difference in people's lives and have strived to build my career from an *inside-out* approach. I started in the mental health field and my interests evolved over time, working in public policy, fundraising, and higher education administration—all of which started out positively but lost their luster. In my work as a career and executive coach, I have worked with more than a thousand individuals seeking to improve their professional lives. Most of them came to me at a time when they were unhappy at work, even though they were highly qualified, established professionals in their fields. While each person's situation was different, I identified one human factor that regularly keeps people from pursuing more satisfying work opportunities: fear. And it shows up in several ways.

Throughout the next nine chapters, this book will illustrate and explore the most common, fear-driven obstacles that show up when someone considers the possibility of a job change or career transition.

Unfortunately, career satisfaction or happiness has not always been seen as a top priority, and sometimes for good reason. For example, during the Depression era of the 1930s, people were simply grateful to have a job that put food on their tables and a roof over their heads. To wish for anything further beyond the basics from a job was considered frivolous.

The norm established by that brand of basic practicality has been passed through the generations, in both overt and subtle ways, to this day. Yet, so many societal elements and economic factors have changed. Standards regarding education, work roles, and career paths have shifted significantly. And with these changes comes an opportunity to do things differently—to explore our options from the inside out. We need to recalibrate our approach to work and careers in order to establish a clear path to our present and future well-being.

The Gallup Organization's[2] research on employee engagement, conducted for decades across hundreds of thousands of companies, reports that only 36 to 39 percent of workers feel engaged in their work. Of the 61 percent who reported feeling disengaged, 14 percent are actively disengaged, meaning they have miserable work experiences, even going as far as to spread their unhappiness to colleagues.

Many of us spend a significant amount of time at work, more than we do with our families, sleeping, and other important parts of life. Our prime working years encompass a substantial portion, about 40 to 50 percent, of our lifetime—perhaps even more. Don't you think our career satisfaction ought to be higher on our priority list?

My intention behind writing this book is to inspire you to consider more meaningful and fulfilling career directions for yourself—*from the inside out.* I want to engage you through the stories of twenty-two people, many of whom generously shared their personal and professional journeys on my weekly podcast, also titled "Work from the Inside Out." Since 2018, I have interviewed more than 175 people about the career transitions they made to gain greater personal and professional satisfaction.

For this book, I selected stories that offer an array of

approaches, illustrating how people pursued meaningful careers. Some of the people profiled faced sudden losses or had a severe accident. In contrast, others experienced a poignant flash of awareness (an aha moment) or had an opportunity that changed their life most unexpectedly. They represent a fascinating variety of roles, industries, and organizations, and many of them eventually became entrepreneurs. While self-employment is just one avenue to career fulfillment, the stories profiled in this book illustrate the iterative nature of navigating our professional lives and how each experience helps us identify and inform the next steps along our journey.

I hope that you will find the stories throughout this book helpful reference points, equipping you to find your way from the *inside out* toward a more satisfying work life. In that spirit, I offer you some words of caution. You may find yourself making comparisons between your career, background, or situation with the scenarios in this book. It might be tempting to assume these stories are models for duplication to accomplish similar results for yourself. Rather than trying to mirror others' achievements, I recommend that you allow their experiences to focus your lens as you envision your next steps, from the *inside out*.

You can read the chapters in this book in any order, according to your interests and needs. To familiarize you with the different perspectives presented, a summary of the chapters follows. Each chapter focuses on one of the nine common obstacles that keep people from pursuing more meaningful career paths. There, you will find an initial discussion of the obstacle, followed by related stories of professionals who found more satisfying work, and a summary of the chapter, ending with reflective questions and guiding activities that you can complete to support your journey. I suggest that you commit to any chapter, read it in total, and follow through with the questions and activities. You will achieve better outcomes if you engage thoroughly with this book rather than just read it.

Chapter 1: Fear: Friend or Foe?

Fear is the theme that is threaded throughout this book, as it is the foundation for what keeps people from taking risks and making changes, including actions that will improve their lives. This chapter looks at fear through both negative and positive viewpoints, as it can serve to protect or prevent us from living a more fulfilling life. Two stories from podcast guests are shared. One is a former minister who transitioned his career to become an FBI agent. As an agent, he learned how to address fear—his own and that of the criminals he had to engage with in order to bring them into custody. The other story is about a high-profile fitness expert whose fast-paced global career was halted twice by cancer. She recovered but later suffered from panic attacks and fought through her fears of "not being perfect enough." These are significantly contrasting stories about fear and career transitions. The chapter ends with suggested activities, such as writing prompts for journaling and reading the book, *Taming Your Gremlin*[3] by Richard Carson.

Chapter 2: It's Never Too Late

This chapter addresses ageism, primarily the limiting beliefs which people impose on themselves. They think they have missed an arbitrary deadline, or they are afraid to try something different, using their age as a reason for not pursuing opportunities or trying new things. Three stories are shared about people who started new careers at ages forty, fifty, and fifty-eight. The narrative and examples also illustrate how one can move around the challenges of ageism in the marketplace. The scenarios in this chapter depict people who were generally less fearful of attempting new careers, demonstrating how changes can be made at various stages in life. One story does focus on the anxiety around networking—showing how the person broke through to conquer it and landed a new career. The chapter ends with guiding questions to provoke self-reflection and suggested activities to build confidence, gain perspective, and get into action.

Chapter 3: Too Many Responsibilities

This chapter is for people who have a deep sense of responsibility for taking care of others, usually family. Typically, they fear that making a career or job change would put their family at financial risk, or would jeopardize the lifestyle they value. Their job satisfaction often takes a backseat to the other people and things they are supporting. This chapter also notes how parents are introducing the world of work and modeling career decisions for their kids during their formative years. Two stories—about a two-parent family and a single-parent family—are presented to show how they made career changes that gave them deep fulfillment while taking care of their responsibilities. In each case, when things didn't go exactly as they had planned, they had no regrets about their choices. The end of the chapter offers guiding activities and reflective questions to help you consider your next steps.

Chapter 4: Careers Are Not Formed in a Straight Line

This chapter attempts to dispel some of the common assumptions and expectations that many of us grow up with about how our professional lives are supposed to proceed: go to school, graduate, get a job, get promoted, retire. This is over-simplified here, but that is the pattern that is generally presented to us. Two stories are shared here that take us on the twists and turns of career journeys as they more often proceed: crossing over sectors and industries, experiencing unemployment, making mistakes, and learning from them—while contributing to more satisfying, fulfilling career choices farther down the path. The chapter ends with a framework for reflection on past experiences to inform what worked/didn't work as a basis for further goal setting and action planning.

Chapter 5: Don't Default to What You're Good At

This chapter draws on the experiences of many readers. They defaulted to a career path based on what everyone told them their strengths were, because doing so seemed like a good idea. Except they discovered years later that their career wasn't a good fit. Sometimes the road to dissatisfaction looks different, in that they grow tired of a vocation they once enjoyed, and it is time for a change; but most people seek a route in which they have strong competencies, with less regard for how much they do or don't enjoy using those skills. The stories here are of two individuals who were very successful in their careers, but their commitment to the work dwindled over time. We learn how they made strategic decisions, implemented changes, and found their way to new jobs that fit them like a glove. The chapter ends with reflective questions and guiding activities to help you clarify your preferences.

Chapter 6: Success Is Not a Destination

This chapter explores the idea that our assumptions and definitions of success dictate the choices we make about our careers and how we conduct our lives. We create contexts for success based on values that may or may not be tied to our sense of fulfillment, satisfaction, and purpose. The stories offered here highlight the career trajectories of three people who made distinct choices to align their work with their goals, sense of purpose, and values. The chapter closes with reflective questions and guiding activities that lead you to envision and clarify the context for what is most important to you.

Chapter 7: You Need to Network, but Not Just for a Job

Networking is essential to career growth and transitions. In addition to making connections and building relationships, an additional context for networking is emphasized: the search for information to better understand the marketplace and drive strategic decisions and choices. Expanding the scope of networking as a "research project" serves the person engaged in a career transition so that they will remain curious, open-minded, and in a learning mindset as they determine their next moves. Two people's stories are included in this chapter: one is an introvert, and the other is an extrovert. Each has extensively and intentionally used networking to expand their professional opportunities. The chapter closes with reflective questions and guiding activities that you can implement to grow and engage your networks and increase your access to relevant information for making better decisions.

Chapter 8: I'm Not Qualified. Do I Belong Here?

Some people stop themselves from pursuing intriguing opportunities, because they believe they are unqualified and do not have a reasonable chance to secure an interview. This chapter is for those who doubt their skills, credentials, qualifications, and potential to be considered for the jobs they find most interesting. Two powerful stories are shared about individuals who demonstrated how they stepped into professional opportunities without formal degrees or prior experience. Were they lucky? Yes, and the lucky people are those who show up in the first place. The chapter ends with a blend of questions and exercises to help you better understand yourself and your potential.

Chapter 9: Uncertainty Is a Fact of Life

This chapter addresses the notion of uncertainty as a fact of life rather than something that only happens to other people. The stories included here illustrate how three individuals emerged from life-threatening and traumatic events to create more meaningful, fulfilling careers. While their stories are uniquely inspiring, the message in this chapter is to ignite readers to action in their lives instead of waiting until "things settle down." The chapter ends with an exercise that helps you to envision their next steps for a satisfying career transition.

Resources

This is a carefully curated appendix that includes recommended books, websites, podcasts, organizations, and other resources that can help you move closer to your goals.

As you read the stories and explore the themes throughout this book, I encourage you to stay open, curious, and alert to opportunities within your reach. Be aware of narrowing thoughts that convince you that *only other people can accomplish those things.* Notice how logical your thinking can be and how easily your aspirations, interests, and joys can end up on the back burner. Throughout the book, you will see yourself reflected in places, while some stories will give you a fresh perspective. Take time to engage with the reflective questions and guiding activities at the end of each chapter to clarify your motivations. They are a tool to spark your thinking toward more meaningful and fulfilling pathways in your work life.

Discuss your thoughts and ideas with other trusted, *positive* people in your life. Those conversations usually offer fresh ideas and energy to move toward your goals.

It is within your control to create a life and make a living that satisfies and gives you greater meaning. I wrote this book to inspire, inform, and open you up to parts of yourself that can *make the impossible possible,* from the *inside out.*

Nothing is impossible, the word itself says I'm possible.

— Audrey Hepburn

1

FEAR: FRIEND OR FOE?

Fear defeats more people than any other one thing in the world.

—Ralph Waldo Emerson

My great uncle Phil, my father's favorite uncle, would say, "Don't worry ahead of time about crossing the bridge. You will figure out what to do when you get there."

He was generally a quiet man, but when Uncle Phil spoke, we listened—his wisdom always landed with us.

When new clients come to me for career transition coaching, they have many questions, but this is one of the most common:

"I know you can't give me a definite answer but…how long does the process usually take before someone clarifies their next move or lands a job?"

My answer: "It depends…"

What would Uncle Phil say? He'd probably say, *I don't know. Just get started and you'll know you arrived when you get there.* In other words, as much as we want to know what is on the other side of the bridge beforehand, the only way to find out what's there is by crossing it. Fear of the unknown and the urgent need to know what is going to happen ahead of time is a common experience for many people who are starting something new. Yet, those fear-based thoughts can limit our view of the options, and leave us feeling helpless.

I believe that fear underlies many of our internal narratives, beliefs, behaviors, and choices; and during career transitions, fear can run rampant. While it can create bottlenecks if not complete blockages that hamper our quality of life, fear is a double-edged sword. It can also induce us to take risks that we will never regret, or it can keep us in a holding pattern that feels safe, but also stuck in the mud.

The purpose of this discussion is to shine a light on how fear is often our enemy, how it can be sneaky, and how we can take control to build a more satisfying path forward.

I don't mean to totally condemn our fears as they can help us to weigh our options and make thoughtful choices. The key is to recognize when our fears block us from making positive choices—when they are disguised as logical thinking, but will actually keep you stuck in an unhappy or stagnant situation.

How do we know when we are being held back versus taking a thoughtful, responsible or creative approach to a big decision?

First, we need to trust ourselves. As we approach unfamiliar territory—for example, a new job or project—we usually want assurances that our efforts will yield positive results, or at least, that nothing negative will happen. When we realize that we do not have a crystal ball to predict the outcome, we immediately leap to doubting ourselves. This spirals into a stream of thoughts about our shortcomings and weaknesses—as well as stories we make up about what others will say or think about us. At times, these thoughts are quite subtle, running beneath the surface of our psyche even when we are generally confident and have had a solid career up to that point.

How we respond to new experiences is not exactly the same for everyone. We want to feel competent in handling new challenges as they arise, and to be able to address them. Most of us want to feel as if we have everything under control and are ready for whatever comes next. While these are instinctively normal desires, they are essentially unrealistic expectations, as we cannot truly know what tomorrow will bring.

So...that said, it is helpful to understand what fears or doubts may show up as we engage in this process of career transition: expanding our knowledge, understanding our options, considering new pathways, making decisions, and then, acting on those choices.

The following stories illustrate two distinct scenarios: how fear is addressed when it is observed from an external view and how fear can be sneaky festering within, sometimes creating debilitating anxiety.

Chip Massey

One of my favorite career transition stories to share is that of my colleague, Chip Massey. Not only is his journey fascinating, but he is one of the kindest and most inspiring people I have ever known. Chip and I met in Dorie Clark's Recognized Expert™ community and once I learned about his professional history, I immediately invited him to be a guest on my podcast "Work from the Inside Out".

Chip's work experience began early in life, growing up on his family's dairy farm near Dover, Delaware, where he held a neighborhood paper route and a job in a local video store as a teen. In college, he studied criminal justice and was drawn to careers that would enable him to help people; he considered the options of going to law school or seminary.

Chip's interest in the Methodist ministry won out. He attended seminary and landed on Maryland's eastern shore, serving two churches for six and a half years.

> I enjoyed getting to know people at that level. It's one of the most profound experiences you can have. People trust you with what they're dealing with and what's going on in their lives. You're seen in the community as somebody who they trust, can go to with problems, who actually listens and cares. Seminary prepares you with various counseling courses to deal with people in crisis, but it's not until you are with them as they are going through heart-wrenching life stuff that you experience how resilient they are.

While Chip deeply enjoyed his work as a minister, he began to feel an internal stirring as if something were missing. He had reflected on a film that had been particularly compelling to him, *Mississippi Burning*, which told the story of two FBI agents who were assigned to investigate the disappearance of a group of civil rights workers in a small Mississippi town. Chip loved the social justice implications of the film and the power behind having a government entity devoted to attacking evil. By his fifth year in the ministry, that restlessness constantly stirred within him, and he knew that it was time for him to make a change.

Minister Chip Massey decided to apply to the Federal Bureau of Investigation (FBI) to become an agent. However, it's important to note that this wasn't a decision made lightly, nor was it based solely on a moment of inspiration.

> I felt in my heart that I wanted something more. And when I say something more, if I broke it down, I wanted a little bit of excitement that

wasn't present in my current life, that was different. There was something almost granular within me that needed a shift. I was in the library doing the research, trying to read various books, like, *What Color is Your Parachute?*[1] and business books. I was curious because sometimes people point to a particular book they read that turned the light switch on or a book that helped to guide them through the process of making a transition in a way that they wouldn't have done completely on their own.

Chip started by learning more about what the Bureau did, as he didn't know any FBI agents. He wanted to know what they did on a day-to-day basis, so he asked around and was introduced to a retired agent—and another who was currently in the FBI. Both had great experiences to share and said the job was one of the best things that they had ever done.

The process of applying and getting accepted to the FBI Academy at Quantico took approximately one year. Chip had to commit to a rigorous physical training program to prepare himself for entering the Academy, while maintaining his "day job." He had to endure extensive personal and medical background checks and interviews and then was accepted into the Academy.

Chip knew he could be eliminated at any point during his time there. Many people would leave after their first three days at the Academy, once introduced to the harshest realities of what they could encounter on the job. Chip successfully passed the required standards, completing the Academy in four months. It was an intense experience in which he was constantly monitored and tested to perform under a variety of high-pressure and stressful situations. I asked him why he chose to make this move in his career and what his underlying

motivations were to make it through the rigors and realities of
the FBI Academy.

> I think it was a belief in yourself and commit-
> ment not to quit—the perseverance of your goal
> and what you want to accomplish. You just have
> to keep at it, and in order to do that, you've got to
> believe that you're capable of making that
> happen. I was looking forward to the cama-
> raderie of being a part of a team. In the ministry,
> it's just you; you're on your own. And it's all on
> you. You're separated out from people who don't
> know how to treat somebody in the clergy. I
> wanted to be a part of this organization that did
> so much good.

Chip was assigned to the Washington, DC, field office,
where he worked on espionage cases and foreign counterintel-
ligence. This involved a lot of travel and collaboration with
the Central Intelligence Agency (CIA) to detect spies within
the US from a foreign, hostile power. Chip also worked on
fugitive programs and with the Victim Witness program. His
last squad was as a public corruption agent. He worked with
an elected official who had encountered bribery and other
malfeasance that needed to be investigated.

Chip's experience with the FBI enabled him to perform
quite a variety of different roles. I asked him to share what it
took for him to switch gears into such highly sensitive work.

> There is a learning curve to each violation, yet
> the principles are the same. The foundation of
> any FBI investigation is obtaining the cooperation
> of somebody involved in the criminal aspect of it.
> I need to find out who this person has contact
> with, and what their motivations are. I do a lot of

background investigation into that. I would try to engage people that the subject of the investigation was in contact with. So, it required learning how to talk to people and connect with them, especially when I was working in criminal violations. People don't want to talk about that. They don't want to talk about fear of retribution or fear of being ostracized in the community. Just plain fear. So, it was my job to engage somebody who was inside the criminal organization, but had a smaller role, yet knew what was going on— get them to trust me and to share information about what was happening.

In 2004, Chip transferred to the New York City field office, where he became a team leader. He had more formal opportunities to expand his skills, experience, and responsibilities at the FBI through assignments on special cases, and when he qualified, he could take additional training and earn special certifications. He took a series of highly specialized courses to earn his certification as a hostage negotiator. Chip said this training has helped him in many aspects of his life beyond engagement with kidnappers, violent, agitated people, and others in crisis. His training as a minister was an excellent complement to this work, as it helped him to connect with people who were in pain on many levels. As an agent or negotiator, his job was to help them resolve a problem.

 The skill set that I got as a hostage negotiator involved connecting to people and helping them manage their fears. For example, I'm sitting across from somebody who has been notified they're the subject of an investigation, they get an attorney, and I had to make a connection to that person. What I really had to do is understand the fears that they were going through and put myself in the place of somebody who is facing the possibility of spending time in prison.

Chip used empathy and active listening to understand people's fears and then spoke with them directly about those feelings. He does the same thing today as a coach and consultant in his work with leaders, managers, and executives in the workplace. He claims that if you just look at the conduct or circumstances of what occurred without understanding the underlying fear that is driving someone's actions, you can't help them change their behavior.

 If there is something in your life that you're fearing, and you're not addressing it, you're going to avoid it. If there's a goal that you want to accomplish, and you know the primary direction is through that fear, it's got to be such a strong desire in you to push through that fear, rather than avoid it. Seth Godin says in that lizard brain analogy (limbic system, fight or flight response) that our survival mechanism is to stay away from things that make us uncomfortable, and that makes us fearful, right? It's human nature. We have to make a conscious decision to go through that fear to get to the other side.

As an example, Chip points to the fear we have when we first learn to ride a bike. Most people can relate to this. The experience delivers a powerful implication, because it involves placing our own physical safety in jeopardy, getting on that bike and possibly risking an injury. Yet, that bike also means a new way of living a life. We know it, but we don't understand the full value that exists until we develop and master the skill. It can be frightening to the point of inciting paralysis. Most people recall breaking through that fear to the exhilaration, excitement, and freedom of being able to ride a bike.

After twenty-two years, Chip retired from the FBI and started his own company, Plowshare Communications, so that he could help people in the workplace break through their fears to become the best leaders, business strategists, and team members. He spoke with people about their needs and the problems they were encountering and believed that his skill set would apply in the business community.

Chip engages his clients, including corporate leaders, to construct and fully own a plan that's specifically geared to addressing their fears. Then, he makes sure that they embrace it. He also speaks to groups, sharing communication skills such as active listening and empathy. He uses the template of hostage negotiations to help people improve their workplace relationships, make good decisions under pressure, and create a culture of trust. Chip teaches the in-depth techniques he has mastered on how to deal with our fear, as well as others' fears, to operate from a place of confidence, clear thinking, flow, and connection.

More recently, Chip has partnered in consulting and training with Adele Cehrs, CEO of When and How Agency, a crisis communications and executive development firm. The same skill sets he used in hostage negotiations and crisis communications are extremely effective in helping leaders make rapid and high-quality decisions in times of stress. Chip and Adele also teach a process of how to make superior decisions in varied business environments, either as part of a team or as a sole arbiter.

 When I deal with executives and business owners, I see clearly that there's something blocking them. They haven't identified it, yet they know that they're either at a plateau or they're scared about moving to a higher level. When fear is operative, we hold ourselves small. Our lizard brain (limbic system) starts talking to us: you can't do that, you shouldn't do that, or you don't deserve that. It's going to do everything it can to destroy our efforts and hold us in our place, even though we're miserable. We might hate our boss, and we don't want to make a change because 'at least this is the devil I know, the paycheck is still coming in, and even if it's killing me, I'm still going to do that job.' My role is to help people figure out what fears are holding them back and unpack them intensely. Then we take that knowledge and build a detailed plan for how they're going to get through to the other side beyond that fear.

Petra Kolber

Petra Kolber is a speaker, author, mindset coach, podcast host, DJ, and wellness leader who is known throughout her industry as a beacon of authentic happiness. As a national workshop leader and keynote speaker, she inspires people to stand up for their lives and live profoundly from their hearts. Her work is rooted in the science of positive psychology, and she coaches individuals and teams on how to get unstuck so that they can become unstoppable. In 2018, Petra released her first book, *The Perfection Detox, Tame Your Inner Critic, Live Bravely, and Unleash Your Joy*.[2] Petra has been a consultant and contributor to many national magazines and has been named Fitness Crusader of the Year by *Health* magazine. She has been the face and voice of leading food and fitness companies such as Reebok, Living, Fitness Music, and California Walnuts. As a two-time cancer survivor, she is passionate about waking people up to the precious gift of time. Her mission is to inspire people to move more and fear less, so that they can stretch their dreams, strengthen their courage muscles, and build an inspired life full of joy and gratitude.

Petra's journey began in Liverpool, England, where she lived until she was eighteen. She started her career as a dancer; she was good at it and danced throughout Europe for ten years. In 1983, she moved to Miami, Florida, and continued to dance.

The year before she moved to the US, Petra became familiar with aerobics, initially looking down on it as if her identity and skill as a dancer were far superior. Once she arrived in Miami, she decided to try it again—this time attending a class with a teacher who was also a dancer. Petra warmed up to it.

 I started studying it, never thinking it was going to be a career, and got my aerobics certification. Then I moved to New York City. In my first audition in New York City, I suddenly realized I'm a good dancer, but nowhere near Broadway. I wasn't a singer. I wasn't an acrobat. Luckily, at this time, fitness and aerobics were in their heyday. There was an aerobics workout called step, and I had gone to the very first training by Reebok. It was just serendipitous, like a year ahead of time. Because I had this thing called step aerobics in my back pocket. Even though I wasn't very seasoned, I got hired to the boutique studios quickly. They were desperate for people to teach this thing called step, because nobody knew how to do it.

Five years later, Petra had completely transitioned out of dance and was teaching about twenty-five fitness classes a week all over New York City. She recalls barely having time to eat or drink, subsisting mostly on meal replacement drinks.

Reebok then decided to contract with her to choreograph, lead, and star alongside three Olympians in a series of fitness videos. One of those stars was skater Nancy Kerrigan, who had been notoriously attacked. The videos turned out so well that she continued with Reebok as a master trainer for the next ten years. Petra traveled all over the world, teaching aerobics to thousands of people. She was having the time of her life.

Then, Petra faced what many people would consider the worst-case scenario, not once, but twice. The first time, she discovered an unusual spot on the sole of her foot that concerned her, especially since her livelihood depended so much on her feet. Petra went to a few doctors over a couple of years before one actually told her it was something to be concerned about—a cancer known as melanoma. She temporarily put her career on hold for surgery, and as soon as she could, she returned to work on crutches to deliver lectures. Reebok was completely supportive of her as she attended to her health needs.

Two years later, Petra found a lump on her neck, and she was feeling extremely fatigued. She thought it was due to traveling all around the world with Reebok, and even though the lump had grown, she didn't think much of it. Once she got it biopsied, it came back as Hodgkin's lymphoma. She was asymptomatic and given a positive outlook from the doctors. Petra underwent chemotherapy and radiation treatments. She'd have chemo on Monday and teach a fitness class on Tuesday.

 I would say I did my most fearless living during that time. Because I'd already faced the worst situation. I thought I might be dead in six months, and now I have life. It is the strangest thing to me now that I'm looking back. My classes were packed. I never had any doubt of being supported during that time. I had amazing angels in the nurses, incredible doctors, and amazing friends. I had a career and some crazy willpower that I knew if I kept on moving, and I listened to my body, it was the one thing that was still a constant. I could still get up and teach a class.

While Petra had many people supporting her, she clearly had a strong work ethic. It seemed as if nothing, not even cancer, would stop her. At the beginning of her success with Reebok, Petra had been given a piece of advice that she took seriously. She was encouraged not to lose her own name for the sake of a brand. So, each time Reebok sent her to work at an event, Petra would reach out to the organizer and offer to deliver an extra workshop in her own name. As a result, she was able to secure her own contracts to build her fitness brand with DVDs and her own productions.

After ten years with Reebok, the fitness industry was shifting dramatically, as it moved toward a "harder is stronger" message and boot camp training. Petra was never that person. Yet she tried to move into that market and became increasingly miserable. It was time for a change.

 I had tried to make my fitness career a reflection of society's definition of success; a perfect body, a perfect appearance, perfect health. I was tired of this. Something was missing. I had the luxury of having an income because I had saved my money. So, I took a couple of years and went back to school to study positive psychology. This was the missing link. I created a program called Moving to Happiness. I took the positive psychology approach of not looking at the body but looking at what is going on between the ears. That's how

I began to move into speaking and writing. While I still am in the fitness industry to a small extent, I speak on the movement not as the end game, but as a vehicle that we can use to become our best self, and fitness is just a piece of that story.

It should not come as a surprise that when Petra finally slowed down and refocused, two deeply personal realizations surfaced. One was the insight that she'd always felt she needed to be a perfect fitness expert. Second, Petra had been suffering from chronic panic attacks for seven years. They didn't occur at the beginning of her career, she assumed because she was not widely known. Yet, her rise to success as a fitness expert felt sudden, once she received so many opportunities to appear on TV in front of thousands of people.

> No one had ever told me that I needed to be perfect to be a great expert, but somewhere in my memory banks my dance coaches from the past told me you're never going to make it, you're not smart enough, you're not enough of this or that. And so those stories started to rear their head, and then I held the idea that to be an expert, I should know everything, I should look a certain way. I then put this internal pressure on myself. This grew into regular, increasing panic attacks, and the long story is that as they grew my world became smaller. I started turning down work.

At that point, Petra was consulting for *Health* magazine. She would be called for a role as contributor on the *Today Show* (NBC) or CBS News, yet she made excuses that she was already booked. Then one day, CBS called, inviting her farther ahead of time than usual to do a fitness segment for New Year's resolutions. Once again, she declined the offer, but the truth was that her calendar was wide open. But something different happened that day. Petra pushed past her fear, picked up the phone, and called them back—pretending that she had made room in her schedule. Next, she contacted her old therapist to get the support she needed to prepare for a return to national TV. It had been five years….

 I showed up. It wasn't perfect. It was good enough that for the next two years, I was the regular fitness expert on their show, and we had a great time. I realized that when I thought people wanted perfection, it was actually keeping me from inspiring them, because they don't connect to perfection. That was the beginning of the journey. And then, when I was doing smaller keynote speaking gigs, I started to share my journey with fear and anxiety.

Petra found that sharing her struggles resonated with audiences. They would approach her and encourage her to write a book. She decided to write about "how do we overcome this idea of having to be perfect?" Alongside that, Petra wanted to make an impact in the wellness industry. She had already been approached by the online education company, Creative Live, to record a course. Six months later, she had completed her positive psychology certification, and then she recorded her program, "Moving to Happiness."

 I've learned the most when things go wrong. We get to look at that through the lens of appreciation versus judgment. When we expect so much from ourselves, we need to know everything, we have to show up perfectly, and so—if we do make a mistake—we are so horrified by it, we don't even look at it as learning. We throw all of that information out, when in fact, if we look at the mistake, 85 to 95 percent of it was a myth. When people own their mistakes and learn from them, there's tremendous integrity in that. That's what really attracts and engages people. It's not the mistake itself. If you try to hold on so tightly, to avoid anything going wrong, you are going to set yourself up for anxiety.

In addition to her courses and speaking, Petra fulfilled a long-term desire that showed up in her life unexpectedly. She became a DJ. Her connection to music as a dancer was deeply rooted.

During her book launch party, she was asked in an interview, "Now that you have written a book, what's next for you?"

Her answer? "I've always been interested in DJing."

Petra's mentor, who she had worked with as a spokesperson for his fitness company, overheard this conversation. Coincidentally, he happened to be a phenomenal DJ.

He asked her "How serious are you?"

Petra said, "I'm very serious."

He said, "Okay, that's all I need to know."

Then a woman Petra knew for over fifteen years approached her. She was the vice president of one of the biggest fitness companies in the country, and she asked Petra the same question, "How serious are you?"

Petra's response was the same, "Very serious."

The woman said, "OK, a year from now, you will DJ our VIP party at our convention with 500 people."

That January, Petra received the invitation that said: VIP party, DJ'd by Petra Kolber. That announcement motivated her. Petra stated that without the mentor and the accountability of the event, she would have given up on her dream. Her mentor helped her during the planning process by having her rehearse over and over—rather than relying solely on her perfectly curated playlist. In Petra's words, the event was *magical*, because she was *present in the moment* and *not trying to be perfect*. This moved her to create a new keynote called "How to Lead Like a DJ, Your Top 10 Hits for Inspired Leadership." Petra continues to love her work as a DJ.

 I often say to people, perfection is only a word. If your thoughts around being perfect suck the joy out of you, then look at how you can reframe what it means to you, and what success means to you. You will probably work just as hard, if not harder, but it's rooted in possibility, creativity, and opportunity—versus fear, dread, and horror of the thought of making a mistake. The atmosphere you are creating is one of pain and mistrust. It is one where people feel they cannot make a mistake, and no one does their best work. Most certainly, they're not being perfect in that context.

As you consider a career transition, it is important to be equipped with techniques for dealing with your doubts and fears when they surface, so that you can be attentive to new information, consider the possibilities and make thoughtful decisions. As Chip and Petra demonstrated, the key to moving beyond fear is to understand its presence and have a plan to work through it. You need a set of approaches to help you maintain an open and curious mindset so that you have confidence as you evaluate your options. While your fears and doubts will try to tell you there are no good choices, you will know differently! As a result, you will be more skillful in assessing and refining your options, so that you can make more focused decisions, that are aligned with your values.

All along the way, fear-based thoughts will show up and may try to stop you in your tracks, sometimes to the point of creating analysis paralysis—wherein you can't make decisions, or revert to making reactionary decisions, due to overthinking. The goal is to notice when those patterns occur and to stop them sooner than later so you can shift the direction of your energy and attention.

Fear is the cheapest room in the house. I would like to see you living in better conditions.

—HAFIZ

Reflective Questions and Guiding Activities

You believe it is time for a new job or complete career reinvention, but your head is full of concerns, objections, and self-doubt. It's difficult to think clearly and know where to begin the process. Here's a practice for unpacking your thoughts and finding your way forward. You will notice a similar approach at the end of each chapter, customized to its area of focus.

Self-Assessment

On a scale of 1 (very uncomfortable) to 10 (completely comfortable), what is your general comfort level with embarking on a career transition (new job or career reinvention)?

What does your score mean to you? Be as specific as possible in articulating your feelings and thoughts about what it will mean to you to engage in a career transition.

If your chosen score was two to three points higher than your original score, what would your experience look like in terms of your thoughts, feelings, and activities related to pursuing your career transition?

What activities might you be considering or doing at that higher comfort level? What kinds of information, relationships, or opportunities would become available to you from that place?

What might get in the way or prevent you from elevating your score? Name as many concerns or obstacles as you can.

What actions can you take to raise your comfort level in the next three to six months? Be as specific as possible.

If you have difficulty thinking about your options, speak with a trusted colleague or friend to identify a few ideas.

Here are a few suggested approaches that have proven effective for a multitude of professionals:

Notice All-or-Nothing Thinking

When considering your options, be aware of all-or-nothing thinking. This type of thinking is usually driven by fear, creating an immoveable scenario. Possibilities in the mid-range often exist and can be more attainable. Run your ideas by a trusted person who can do some creative thinking with you. Another way to explore this is by drawing a line on paper, or putting a length of tape on the floor. Put the opposing thoughts at either end of the line and brainstorm ideas of what can occur in between. Try walking and stepping on different sections of the tape, and notice what ideas show up by talking about them as you move.

Reframe Your Thoughts

Reframing is one of my favorite coaching skills. A great example of reframing your perspective happens by asking, "Is the glass half empty, or is the glass half full?" How you frame or think about a situation can significantly alter the way you see it, and in turn, your feelings, decisions and actions would all be transformed. Some of my favorite questions that prompt a reframe are:

- How do I feel when I look at this situation now?
- What do I want instead? How would I like to feel about it?
- What would it take for me to feel THAT way about it?
- What kind of help would I need to get there?

So What!

When you are aware of your fear or doubts, respond with a mental or verbal *SO WHAT!* I know it sounds snarky, but there are times when this can snap you out of a belief or thought that is just not helping you. This falls in line with a worst-case scenario exercise, which can also be helpful when you feel particularly trapped by a fearful line of thinking:

- What is the worst thing that could happen?
- What is the next worst thing that could happen?
- And the next worst thing…?

Journaling

Regular journaling about your thoughts or concerns can help to release any angst associated with it, along with helping you develop ideas for positive action. After each writing session, put the journal aside for a day or two. Review your entry a few days later, and journal a response to yourself. Notice any other thoughts or feelings it evokes and how those relate to your goals.

Beware of Your Gremlins

Read the book *Taming Your Gremlin*[3] by Rick Carson, and practice the art of "Simply Noticing." This book offers the strategies to help you manage the negative self-talk that can hold you back from enjoying your life to its fullest extent. All it takes is practice, practice, practice.

Create a System to Track and Manage Activities.

I encourage all of my clients to create a system, a go-to place where they can keep track of people, contact information, links, important dates, and additional data that helps them to stay focused and organized. Use an approach that works best for you, but start with something, and if it needs to be changed along the way, that's fine. It can be anxiety provoking to begin a career transition and have information scattered in different places. Some of the more common systems that seem to work well are spreadsheets, relational databases, and project management software packages. Check the resources section for specific suggestions.

Ask Yourself: How Can This Be Easier?

When it all begins to feel overwhelming, stop, take a deep breath, exhale, then take another deep breath, exhale, and ask yourself, how can this be easier?

2

IT'S NEVER TOO LATE

When I was five years old, my mother always told me that happiness was the key to life. When I went to school, they asked me what I wanted to be when I grew up. I wrote down 'happy.' They told me I didn't understand the assignment, and I told them they didn't understand life.

—John Lennon

I have heard many clients say, "When you get to my age, it's too late," or "I expected to be farther along in my career by this age." One client shared his fear that he was losing ground and that while considering a career change might be in order, he thought it might be too late already. He was only thirty-eight years old!

Let's examine what some would call the *scarcity mindset* and how it stops us from considering potential opportunities. We believe we have less of something that we need more of, and as a result, are convinced that we lack the resources or qualifications to take action. For example, there's the scarcity of time (age), finances, and the lack of confidence in one's own skills. Perfectionism would fit within this mindset as well. As discussed in the previous chapter, people are driven by fear into a state of paralysis to the point that they end up doing nothing. They assure themselves that their "ship has sailed"; it's a *fait accompli*. Yet, if you are reading this book, you must be looking for another way through. I am here to tell you that there are many ways to answer the questions, "At this juncture in my life, what would I like to pursue? What do I need to learn and once I know more, what would it look like if I were fully engaged in my next role? By when could I expect that step to occur?"

The stories in this chapter are just a few examples of people who pursued career transitions at ages when many people would have dismissed stepping into new professions. While some had the comfort that financial resources provide to help make these dreams happen, they still had to do the hard work, and make a difference because they could, regardless of their age. These are stories of *want-tos* not *have-tos*.

What is your *want-to*? What is stopping you? What are you waiting for?

For many of us a significant part of our identity as adults is defined by our career, or work. Yet how many of us are *being who we want to be*, versus *being who we think others expect or need us to be as professionals*? The harsh reality is, as noted earlier, too few of us are not feeling engaged by our work. If you are concerned that it is too late to find work that is better aligned with your interests and talents, but would like to explore the possibilities, this book is definitely for you.

Arza Goldstein

People like Arza Goldstein inspire me to get out of bed in the morning because she's not afraid to make new things happen in her life. Our kids were in elementary school together, so for the better part of six years, we hung out at school drop-off time, in Starbucks, and in committee meetings. We got to know each other quite well and, during that time, I became a big fan of hers. I was delighted to invite her to be my podcast guest, because examples such as hers inspired me to launch my show in the first place. You see, Arza, at forty, went back to school to fulfill prerequisite requirements in order to qualify for nursing school while raising three young children. I witnessed this part of her journey, in awe of her steady focus and drive to see it through.

Before we go farther ahead, let's see where this all began. After college, Arza spent time looking for work that would capture her interests and passions, which drew her to pursue training and development work because she enjoyed educating people. Shortly thereafter, while her husband was in law school, she pursued a master's degree in training and development. Once she completed her master's, she worked in the sales department of an investment banking consulting firm. Arza learned that she was not comfortable in the "corporate bubble." She then followed her interest in houses and got her real estate broker license, thinking that she could also draw on her recent experience in sales. However, Arza discovered that real estate did not feel right to her either.

 I think there was a disconnect for me in terms of how I felt in my body. I remember having a lot of physical discomfort at some level. It just didn't feel right physically, or emotionally.

Arza tried to fit into several career boxes, and they just didn't feel right. At that time, she also had a full-time job as the mother of two young children (a third one came along later), and she loved it. With clear intentions and reflections, Arza decided to make that her sole occupation for the next several years.

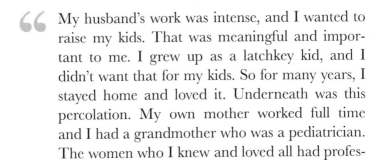

> My husband's work was intense, and I wanted to raise my kids. That was meaningful and important to me. I grew up as a latchkey kid, and I didn't want that for my kids. So for many years, I stayed home and loved it. Underneath was this percolation. My own mother worked full time and I had a grandmother who was a pediatrician. The women who I knew and loved all had professional lives and identities. I felt that something was missing.

Arza had given birth to her third child and felt an "itch" to do something outside the home. It had been a complicated pregnancy, including two months on bed rest. She experienced the medical and emotional elements of high-risk pregnancies. In the process, Arza learned about the supportive role that birth doulas have with women, their partners, and families. It intrigued her so much that she interviewed a few people in the field to learn more and decided to train to become a birth doula.

> Inherently, I am a real caregiver, so that work was appealing and interesting to me. And it was part-time. I was compelled to understand more. I thought birth was an incredible experience.

Once she completed her training and requirements, Arza joined a birth doula group that she worked with for five years. During that time, *the next thing* started percolating in her mind.

And that next thing was becoming a nurse. Once her youngest child was in preschool, Arza began to take the prerequisite courses at the local community college, so that she could qualify for nursing school.

You may wonder what compelled Arza to do all of this simultaneously. She had three young children, worked as a birth doula, and was taking classes at the community college. Oh…and she was just about to celebrate her fortieth birthday.

What was she thinking? At the time, I was a witness to her drive, passion for her work, and her family. I was cheering her on, and I admired her gusto. And yet, I realized that was merely my perception of her ambitions. In our interview, I asked what compelled her to pursue nursing school on top of everything else she was doing at that time in her life.

> Honestly, it was fear. I feared that my life as I knew it might change. And I was afraid that I was going to look back at my life and feel that I hadn't met my potential.

I asked Arza what compelled her to choose such a challenging and layered approach to address her fears, versus just finding a job that she was already qualified to do. She said she had always been a good student and did well in a structured context. Arza also felt that she had the "being home with the kids" skill set handled well—and that she just wanted to pursue something else.

Arza completed nursing school, and as a result of working through the range of required clinical rotations, she decided to specialize in hospice nursing. That choice felt right to her. Just as she had worked as a birth doula, she saw some of the parallels in helping people and their families with end-of-life care. For many years, Arza worked four days a week, while she still had a child in the lower grades. This setup provided the flexibility she wanted to be available at home while completing the significant documentation requirements for the job.

After eleven years as a hospice nurse, Arza made the very difficult decision to leave her job. While she loved her boss and colleagues, she felt her work there was done. She admitted it was hard to leave the structure, and the regular paycheck, but she began to experience those physical and emotional signs that told her it was time for a change.

> You know, I'm a big meditator. So, when I allowed myself to just listen to my internal dialogue, I got a lot more clarity. My work there was done. I said it out loud, and it just made all the sense in the world to me. I wanted to be able to run my own life. And the other thing is I felt strongly that I had a unique skill set to offer—and that I wanted to be paid fairly for it. Those were the two pillars on which I wanted to construct my next chapter.

Arza started an organization with a few other women in Newton, Massachusetts, called Living Wisely Dying Well. Their goal is to get people comfortable talking about their values, goals, and preferences for their end of life.

In addition, Arza established an End of Life Doula practice, in which she helps patients and their families make their remaining time together less stressful and more meaningful. As an End of Life Doula, Arza is able to bridge the gaps between time, services, and advocacy that hospice services cannot provide. She offers highly customized education, pre-hospice planning, accompaniment of individuals and families to appointments, crisis consulting, and bedside vigil support. While she no longer practices under her nursing license, Arza can provide counsel because of her nursing experience. Her unique background allows her to guide her patients in a unique way, especially when they may be reluctant to engage in certain kinds of care or services.

> I am a big believer that when we have death sitting on our shoulder, we live our lives with greater intentionality. The idea of death is a gift

that pushes us to not take things for granted, to say what we need to say, and to do the things we want to do.

As I do with many of my podcast guests, I asked Arza, "What key piece of advice would you offer to someone who's trying to figure out what's next—to step into a new career or other meaningful transition?"

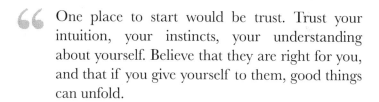 One place to start would be trust. Trust your intuition, your instincts, your understanding about yourself. Believe that they are right for you, and that if you give yourself to them, good things can unfold.

Sally Wovsaniker

My cousin, Sally Wovsaniker, was one of those adults who I recall liking, aka being comfortable with, as a child. She was always kind and engaging, taking an interest in me and my life. Sally was a teacher. I recall her being involved in a wide variety of community activities, often holding leadership positions in those groups. She was married to my Dad's first cousin, Harold, who was an attorney, and they raised two sons during the 1950s through 1960s in Hillside, New Jersey. While teaching, Sally earned her master's degree in education and later another master's degree in guidance, which enabled her to become a guidance counselor.

Sally loved being a student and keeping busy, as evidenced by her active participation in many community groups. She grew up in a family that valued education and intellectual pursuits. I remember Sally's mother, Esther, who often attended family events. Esther had gone to law school, only one of two females in her class, although she never practiced law. She married her law school classmate, Sam Gooen, Sally's father. Since Sally was born in 1929, Esther must have been in law school earlier in the 1920s.

Years later, once Sally and Harold had established their "empty nest"—with one son in college and the other in law school—Sally, at forty-six, decided to go to law school. She continued her work as a guidance counselor during the day and attended law school at night. At fifty, Sally graduated and passed the bar exam. She continued to work as a guidance counselor while practicing law after school into the evenings at Harold's law office. According to her son, Alan, who I interviewed for this story, she offered the most reasonable fees which made her one of the most affordable attorney's in town. She simply loved to help people and organizations with their wills, closings, and other routine legal matters.

Sally was a learner and a giver. Alan told me in jest that until he was twelve years old, he thought she had a phone growing out of her ear. He recalls that she would get home from a day of teaching and call her mother, sister, and best friend to check on them. He said she was always calling people to see how they were doing; she cared for everyone.

What I found noteworthy about Sally is she cared so much for others but also nourished her own desire for learning and engagement with her community. She worked until she was seventy years old.

Keith

Keith (name changed to protect his identity) came to me for career coaching after a twenty-eight-year career in software development and project management in the financial services industry. A few years earlier, he had been laid off from his last full-time role and was working part-time as a project manager for a small nonprofit organization that created and managed affordable housing units in an affluent Boston suburb. The grant that funded his position was ending soon, and he wanted to identify full-time opportunities with benefits that he could transition into, either in an affordable housing organization or a property management role. Keith told me that he needed the income and benefits, but also felt that it was important emotionally for him to be working.

At first glance, Keith appeared to be in his mid-sixties. He was quite shy and reserved in his demeanor, which concerned me, especially when he also expressed serious trepidations about networking. As much as I hate to acknowledge it, ageism is an issue, and combining that with Keith's extremely introverted style seemed like a tall order to fill, given his goal of moving into both a new role and industry.

Somewhere in our conversations, it surfaced that Keith was actually fifty-eight years old. Unfortunately, it was inconsequential that I was wrong about his age. What did matter was the fact that he had minimal experience in the industry he wanted to work in, a very small network, and he was about to become unemployed. The odds were not in his favor. However, he did have a few things that were working for him: he was passionate about getting involved in the field of affordable housing, he was motivated to do the work to get into the field, and he engaged a coach to support and guide him through the process.

The field of affordable housing can include roles as divergent as being a property manager, an urban planner, or a social worker. Keith was sure that it would be unlike anything he had done before. Fortunately, I had previously worked in the public policy arena on issues related to affordable housing and had the benefit of a bird's-eye view of the stakeholders and roles that developed and maintained affordable housing programs.

As a coach, I do not always have the foundational knowledge in an industry or field, but I have acquired a significant degree of information over the years and can access additional resources when needed, based on my extensive network.

The coach does not need to have all of the answers, but they do need to know how to ask the right questions.

Keith and I created a list of a wide array of relevant organizations and collected appropriate job descriptions so that he could begin to get a feel for the work happening locally and where he might see himself fitting in. We also identified a list of individuals who worked in the field or related areas—some of whom were former colleagues of mine—so that Keith could begin to engage in conversations, learn more about their experiences, and get their advice about the next steps he should take in his job search. While I was able to ask my contacts if they would be willing to speak with Keith, the challenging part was getting Keith to follow through and reach out to people. This was a very difficult part of the process for him, as he never had done any networking before, and the process made him extremely uncomfortable. We started slowly with a few people he knew through connections he made in his part-time job, and we built traction from there. In the meantime, Keith began to attend committee meetings at one of the local Community Development Corporations, known as a CDC. CDCs are nonprofit organizations that support and revitalize communities, through economic initiatives and the development of affordable housing. They may also be involved in a wide range of community services that meet local needs—such as adult basic education, job training, financial literacy and other social programs. By getting involved with the CDC, Keith was able to form targeted relationships in a natural way, while giving him more experience with the development of affordable housing.

Over several months, Keith eased into making more networking contacts with a variety of affordable housing and urban planning professionals who were very helpful in pointing him to resources, organizations, and additional people he could speak with about his career goals. At the same time, Keith got involved with another local nonprofit organization that was raising money to develop affordable housing, and he became the president of their board of directors. He built a solid network, while gaining the experience and visibility he needed to be credible in the field. He began to apply and interview for positions that leveraged his project management skills. It was a stressful process even though he was doing all the right things along the way. He was making great connections, getting referred into organizations, being invited for interviews, and getting asked to return for additional rounds of interviews. Still, he had many rejections, which took its toll on his confidence. Our coaching sessions were instrumental in keeping his process (and psyche) moving forward positively and productively.

Keith's persistence and investment in the networking and coaching process paid off. Six months from the start of our coaching engagement, he landed a wonderful program management role with an urban housing authority. We have kept in touch over the years, and he was enormously happy there. He has since retired and still serves as a volunteer board member for several organizations.

I share Keith's journey here because he needed to chip away through several obstacles to achieve his goal. Seeking a new functional role while moving into a new industry along with his reticence to engage in networking, at his age were all challenging factors to overcome. The key to his successful outcome was his ability to persevere through his discomfort with networking and consistently engage in conversations, ask for advice, and get the information he needed to reach the opportunities he wanted.

When someone is concerned about how their age will be perceived as a job candidate, networking becomes critically important. This is a big issue for a workforce that is working longer as people enjoy better health, need to earn income, and want to remain productive. I have worked with clients in their seventies to help them achieve full-time employment. It's not easy nor simple, yet it is completely possible.

I want to acknowledge some of the typical and paradoxical challenges that older job seekers face repetitively. It can be very draining to find a workaround to these roadblocks, yet with the right support, key steps in place, and a lot of patience, it is entirely possible to move forward into a satisfying, meaningful work situation. Let's consider an employer's potential objections or questions around these situations, and how to work around them in the application process.

You are overqualified. Dorie Clark, author of *Reinventing You*[1], suggests that you get ahead of any question on this topic and say, "You might wonder how I'd respond to being managed by someone younger than me, when I used to manage a large staff. That's exactly why I want this job—and part of the value I bring. Having been a manager, I understand the pressures and frustrations they face, so I can be an even better employee. And I'm eager to learn about this new area from someone with real expertise in it."

You will want a higher salary. Many of my clients have expressed a willingness to earn less once their nest has been emptied and their retirement savings is stabilized. Unfortunately, there is not an eloquent way to tell an employer that you are willing to accept a lower salary, other than to make it explicitly clear that you understand the position pays less than what you were previously earning, and you are completely OK with that. If you were introduced to the employer through a mutual connection, you may find the opportunity to convey that message more easily during the initial conversation. The employer needs to understand what your goals and intentions are, so that they can assess your fit and value against the company's goals.

Your knowledge of technology may be out of date. Take online classes to stay current, keep your LinkedIn profile up-to-date, and maintain a consistent and engaging professional presence on social media.

Will you have the energy to keep up? Take a leadership role in your community, join a board, chair a committee, make your mark, stay active and be engaged.

Ageism exists everywhere, and yet, it is difficult to confront directly. To prevent ageism from taking over, I recommend staying connected to resources in your community, online, or through your networks to support your search efforts. The possibilities are there, if you remain open and positive.

You are never too old to set another goal
or to dream a new dream.

—C.S. LEWIS

Reflective Questions and Guiding Activities

It is understandable that your age and associated factors create doubts when considering a career transition. The key to moving through and beyond those obstacles is to create a step-by-step plan that enables you to see the possibilities and make progress within smaller, individual components. Our tendency is to think in all-or-nothing terms. This is where the walls go up and block our view of what is truly possible.

Self-Assessment

On a scale of 1 (very uncomfortable) to 10 (completely comfortable), what is your general comfort level with embarking on a career transition (new job or career reinvention) at this time?

> What does your score mean to you? Be as specific as possible in articulating your feelings and thoughts about what it means to you to engage in a career transition at this time.

> If your chosen score was two to three points higher than your original score, what would your experience look like in terms of your thoughts, feelings, and activities related to pursuing your career transition?

> What activities might you be considering or doing at that higher comfort level? What kinds of information, relationships, or opportunities would become available to you from that place?

What might get in the way or prevent you from elevating your score? Name as many concerns or obstacles as you can.

What actions can you take to raise your score in the next three to six months? If you have difficulty thinking about your options, speak with a trusted colleague or friend to percolate a few ideas.

Here are some suggested activities that you can try to move your professional journey forward:

Get More Information

Whenever we start something new, we usually require more information. In thinking about your career interests, what questions are on your mind? Public libraries are fantastic resources for all kinds of information. Get acquainted with the reference librarians and ask them to show you how to obtain answers to the questions you are probably asking yourself right now. Some libraries will give you printed reports with the information you need as part of the services they deliver to the public. Larger city libraries may offer more services and programs that are often available to non-residents as well.

In addition to libraries, there are many other sources for information such as professional associations and networking groups, people you will connect with during informational interviews and other informal conversations, professional and trade publications and the internet. Leave no stones unturned!

Join a Job Seeker Group

In many communities there are well organized job seeker groups, sometimes hosted by local libraries, which serve as a good way to get connected with other people, information, and ideas about careers and the job market. Additionally, search the internet to see if there are other programs or services in your area that help job seekers in your community. Many of these programs are geared toward assisting older job seekers.

Build Your Skills

There are many low-cost options for learning new skills and expanding your knowledge. Online courses taught by university professors and skilled professionals, community-based adult education courses, and local universities all offer affordable, high-quality educational opportunities that can help you stay current on your skills and increase your reach into the job market. See the Resources section for a selected list of programs.

Recommended reading:

Working Identity: Unconventional Strategies for Reinventing Your Career[2], by Herminia Ibarra

Based on her in-depth research on professionals and managers in transition, Ibarra outlines an active process of career reinvention that leverages three ways of "working identity": experimenting with new professional activities, interacting in new networks of people, and making sense of what is happening to us in light of emerging possibilities.

3

TOO MANY RESPONSIBILITIES

*Become a possibilitarian. No matter how dark things seem to be
or actually are, raise your sights and see possibilities—always see
them, for they're always there.*

—Norman Vincent Peale

It's one thing to consider a dream as just that: *a dream—*
something that is deeply desired, but still feels elusive, as if it
would never be possible. Sometimes a dream is something you
wish for out in the distance that you might consider possessing
in reality one day—somehow, someway, sometime, maybe...if
at all. Or a dream might be something that you really want
and can begin to consider, yet with no strings attached or
expectations.

So how about we begin considering if we can achieve that
dream, and if so, how to make it happen? Can you start where
you are?

You have responsibilities; the list is long and full. The list
has demanded of you financially and relationally over many

decades: children to raise, mortgage or rent to pay, tuition to save, vacations to take, cars to maintain, medical expenses, retirement savings, emergency funds, elderly care, and on and on. How could you possibly consider yourself and make changes that might jeopardize your ability to attend to all of those people counting on you and matters of importance?

I commend you and respect your deep sense of loyalty and responsibility. I do not say that lightly, as there are many important things in life that we choose to put before our own needs or desires. And there are many times when we absolutely must prioritize others ahead of us. However, there are other ways to look at this, and that is what this chapter will address. You know how when you get on an airplane and they go through the safety speech? They tell you about the oxygen supply and how the masks will come down in case of emergency. The instructions are very clear that you should help yourself first, and then help others—including your children. Why do they tell you that?

Because you need to put your oxygen mask on first in order to help anyone else.

So, if you are in a situation where you are feeling stuck because you believe you must stay where you are due to the responsibilities and obligations you hold so dear, I ask you to think again.

Ask yourself: *Is that really true? Am I 100 percent sure? Is there another way?*

Mark Dyck

Mark Dyck has made several, as he puts it, "uncommon choices" in his life. He grew up in Regina, Saskatchewan, Canada—a small city, population 200,000, in the middle of the prairies. Like so many of us, he was raised with well-intentioned messages about how to live the "good life": go to school, get a good job, keep your head down and work for thirty years, then you'll get a pension and be fine. Mark's folks ran a small gas station franchise, and his dad was an auto mechanic. They didn't want him to follow the same path they had taken. Mark attended university, feeling unattached to a particular area of study, so he floated around until he started getting good grades in computer science and statistics. As he states it, he kind of *fell into* becoming a computer science major and earned his degree. Mark went through his university's co-op program, where he completed work placements along the way. His final placement was with the provincial telecommunications company, which then hired him to stay on after graduation. The plan, which had been laid before him by his parents, was working beautifully. Mark was on the road to the good life. He had a degree, a steady paycheck, and shortly thereafter, he got married. He and his wife, Cindy, then started a family.

 I stayed and I worked and got a steady paycheck and that was all there was.

They decided that Cindy would stay home with the children, yet Mark felt as if he were missing all the fun. Mark figured that many women were asking for part-time hours when they had young children at home, so why not a man? So, he negotiated with his employer to reduce his hours to a four-day workweek. He was the first male in his company to work a reduced schedule. Mark was really good at his job. Even though his degree was in computer science, he was much better with people than with technology. Mark excelled at explaining tech to all the clients and different departments. The company wanted him to keep doing that, so he had the leverage to go part-time while making a positive impact on the company's bottom line.

Then came his next big question, "Is this all there is?" And pretty soon, his wife soon joined him in the chorus.

At the time, Mark was reading Seth Godin's book *Purple Cow: Transform Your Business by Being Remarkable*[1], and it compelled him in a way that he could no longer just stick with the plan.

> That whole idea that we should just keep our heads down and wait for our pension wasn't working for me. So, I said, 'Well, I really want to make something amazing and do something remarkable.'

Mark had an idea. They didn't have good bread in town, and he was starting to get really fascinated by baking bread as a hobby. In 2004, Mark was serious enough about his hobby to go to British Columbia on summer vacation to learn how to build a brick oven from Australian Alan Scott, one of North America's master brick oven makers. Two years later, he took another summer vacation to start building a brick oven in his backyard, spending a year to complete it on the Fridays he was away from work. Fridays then became his baking days; Mark started to sell bread to friends and neighbors on the weekends. His bread became very popular, and demand grew quickly.

Four years later, Mark and Cindy were carefully considering taking the leap to open up their own bakery. Mark did everything he could to go into this situation with his eyes wide open—visiting other bakeries, joining the Bread Bakers Guild of America, and talking with as many people as he could. He hit the road and visited small bakeries that were within a day's drive, sometimes even staying overnight at the baker's house. He'd even go in at four in the morning and bake for a shift with them before driving home. Mark gathered a lot of advice.

In 2011, Mark and Cindy opened the Orange Boot Bakery, a neighborhood artisan bread bakery in their hometown of Regina, Saskatchewan. It was the first and only artisan bread shop in town. According to Mark, it quickly became popular—with people coming out of the woodwork through word of mouth—and they never did any paid advertising.

> We were busy on our first day. We just ran like crazy people that didn't know what we were doing. I think as we got going, I realized that the joy I got out of it was the connection with people, more than what I was doing. We were using local flour and we were trying to be a positive force in the community. I think when you're in the middle of it—it's just, I can say that I actually built this thing.

But let's be clear here. This was not all rainbows and unicorns.

Five years into running the bakery, Mark and Cindy were feeling burnt out as they were working late nights, early mornings, and had little time to connect directly with their customers. As Mark put it, "the business was running us." At their peak, they had thirteen employees, and that required them to move a lot of product each day. At that juncture, to grow further, they would have needed to scale the business to go into wholesale, and that was not appealing to them.

They tried to find another way to grow the business in a sustainable way. Their baking crew had been with them a few years and they were all very good, but each in their own way was ready for a change. One got married and moved away. Another was just burnt out from baking, because she'd been working in a bakery since she was sixteen and wanted to do something else. Mark and Cindy hired people to replace them who didn't work out, so all of a sudden, they were short-staffed. They limped along and slowly rebuilt the team.

They realized that with their current way of operating, they could never keep the team around long enough to really advance the business—and grow creatively as well. Mark and Cindy planned to take till the end of the year, muddling along. Then they'd close the bakery for a while and get another good team built.

But before that happened, they got a buy-out offer from a coffee shop that wanted to expand into their neighborhood. The shop owner wanted the whole space to be their kitchen. They took the offer with the idea that they would pause the business for a few months, consider their options, and look for other spaces. Once they took that pause, Mark and Cindy realized they were "pretty darn tired."

> Every time I start something new, I get clear about what I want and who I am. Even when I had the bakery, I was like, am I doing this because I want to be a master at this craft, or am I doing it to serve people? And what I've learned is I do things to serve people. You know, the bread was a vehicle to make connections with people.

Once he and Cindy recovered from closing the bakery business, Mark worked as a baker at a small restaurant for a former customer while figuring out what to do next. He enrolled in Seth Godin's altMBA program, which gave him the tools and resources to develop himself and his ideas going forward. He had been thinking about doing a baker's podcast and used his time in the program to plan for it. Mark embraced the altMBA opportunity to work with other entre-preneurially minded people in the program—and was able to get the podcast off the ground.

Today, Mark is focused on his leadership roles as the chief community advocate at *the* Right Company and head coach for The Story Skills Workshop. He also mentors bakers in his online bakers' community and hosts his bakers' Rise Up! podcast. *the* Right Company is an online mentorship community where like-minded business owners support each other to create business strategies that fit their unique vision and goals for building *their* right career or company. They grow personally and professionally by connecting with each other in a safe space and sharing their challenges, experience, and wisdom within the community.

As a coach for The Story Skills Workshop, Mark periodically supports coaches who are helping students worldwide in Seth Godin's Akimbo Workshops to tell engaging stories that persuade, influence, and inspire.

Mark bakes bread on the weekends in his backyard brick oven, selling up to 150 loaves to friends and neighbors. He loves connecting with them and finding out how his community is doing. As much as he enjoys figuring out a new bread recipe or technique, Mark is clear that what really floats his boat is interacting with people.

 My advice with transitions is you're going to have to make a leap of faith. You can cover your bases as much as you can, but you can't live with one foot in both worlds forever. I got a leave of absence for a year to start the bakery. I honestly thought, 'I could get this running and it'll run on its own, so I can go back and do the other job.' There was no possible way, but I needed to know that I had a little bit of a safety net there. I'm guessing there are a lot of people who might not consider it an option to even ask their employer for a leave of absence to give them a feeling like they would have something to go back to, should something not go in the right direction.

Stacey Altherr

Facebook has a way of pulling us into a time-space continuum, whether we like it or not. It can be fun to catch up with people and see what is happening in their lives, but more often it can suck you into a mindless vortex for long periods of time. Still, there have been a few fortunate times when I connected with an old friend or classmate, and it was truly an enjoyable experience. Without Facebook, many of these connections would have never occurred. I am so glad I paid attention to what my old childhood classmate Stacey Altherr had been doing, as I found her story to be incredibly inspiring.

Stacey and I grew up in the same neighborhood on Long Island in New York. After high school, our lives went in different directions. Fast forward forty years (yikes!), and technology brought us back together.

I learned that Stacey had become an investigative journalist for *Newsday*, the major daily newspaper on Long Island. After putting herself through college, she signed up with a temp agency and was assigned for two weeks at *Newsday*.

> The first day, I was overwhelmed by being in a newsroom. It was really loud. A lot of people were screaming and some even cursing. Basically, they just seemed like grouchy people barking orders at me. At the end of the day, I said to the manager of the clerks, thank you so much for this opportunity, but I really don't think this is for me. She looked me in the eye and said, 'Come back tomorrow.' For some odd reason, I did. I ended up staying for thirty years.

Stacey worked her way up from answering phones and clerking to working in the photo department, later doing research for all of the big news projects. Eventually, she settled in as a reporter, where she covered government and features, which she found to be a very fulfilling career.

As a single woman, Stacey was able to dedicate a lot of her life to a career she loved. She was always available and happy to do whatever they needed at the newspaper. But in 2009, Stacey traveled to Russia to adopt an eight-year-old boy, and life became more complex. As an investigative journalist, her job demanded that she be responsive to breaking news stories. As a single parent of a child who was adjusting to a whole new reality, Stacey had taken on the biggest job of her life. She was able to make some adjustments in her role at work to accommodate her parenting responsibilities, but her situation between work and home remained demanding.

 One of the things that I've learned in life is that it's OK to struggle for a little while if there's a goal at the end. But if you're struggling and you don't really see a goal, it's time to move on, and it's OK to move on.

After three years of planning, Stacey left *Newsday* and freelanced for a while. She wanted to move to a warmer climate and always loved Florida. So, she asked her son, who was heading into high school at the time, what he thought about moving. They decided to do it with the caveat that if either one was miserable, they could return to New York.

Since Stacey is a researcher by nature, she started looking into school districts, and calling people she knew who lived in certain areas of Florida, narrowing the search down to two communities. She found that people were very welcoming when she went down there to look at schools with her son. They met other new families on the school tours, and they exchanged email addresses and kept in contact with one another. Over the next few months, they collected and shared information, and encouraged their kids to connect through social media so they could have a little community of their own.

For the first time since she was fourteen years old, Stacey decided not to work. She dedicated her focus on the move to Florida.

 I just kind of relaxed, enjoyed my new surroundings, and helped my son get settled in. That was really important to me. So right away, he went into football, and I signed him up for two summer camps to get him around other kids. I was lucky I could do that. Then I started to try to figure out what I was going to do with the rest of my life.

Stacey recalls being in her twenties and talking to a friend about how she wanted to open a tea shop, even before tea shops were a big deal. And throughout the thirty years of her fast-paced career in which she worked very closely with colleagues, she would often say that she was going to "open a coffee shop and pour coffee for people" when she left Newsday. Yet, when Stacey moved to Florida, she had no intention of buying a business. She had never owned a business before and thought she would do freelance writing, and see if she could get a job.

Then one day Stacey was fooling around on the internet, and it led her to a site that listed businesses for sale. She noticed a listing for a cafe on Longboat Key, located a half-hour from her home, and seeing the ad took Stacey right back to her dreams. Before she could hesitate, she emailed the owner, and they invited her to come by with no obligation. So just like that, Stacey went to look at it, and within a few days, she looked at her finances. Periodically, they are stricken with red tides where she lived, which are harmful algal blooms that occur when microscopic algae multiply to higher-than-normal concentrations, causing toxic conditions that kill marine life and cause respiratory illness in humans. So, it was a risk to go into business in that location on the Gulf Coast.

Despite this, Stacey decided that life was too short not to try something she really wanted to do. She moved forward and put all her efforts into running the cafe.

Stacey was fortunate that the previous cook stayed on with her. She immediately connected on LinkedIn and Facebook groups with other restaurateurs and asked a lot of questions: *How does one run a cafe? What do you do when the servers walk out the first day you take ownership of a cafe during high season?* Yup…it happened.

After the initial speed bumps, Stacey had things up and running smoothly. She also saw the opportunity to share some life lessons with her son.

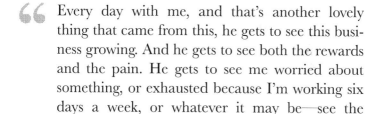

> Every day with me, and that's another lovely thing that came from this, he gets to see this business growing. And he gets to see both the rewards and the pain. He gets to see me worried about something, or exhausted because I'm working six days a week, or whatever it may be—see the rewards. He's proud of the business.

Two years into the business, Stacey had her first confrontation with red tide and had to close the cafe for several months due to water contamination and additional public health issues. As a safeguard, Stacey had continued to pick up freelance writing jobs as a journalist while running the café. She was able to increase her assignments once the red tide hit. While she was as prepared as possible for these challenges, it was still a very stressful time. And it was not the only time she had to deal with this problem. Stacey encountered red tide again within a year of that first occurrence.

But that wasn't the only challenge. Less than a year later,

the COVID-19 pandemic hit.

Stacey felt deeply grateful to have fulfilled her dream as a cafe owner and told me she had no regrets, but as anyone can imagine, she reached a point where it was no longer financially feasible to carry the café, given the amount of time she had to keep it closed. She also wanted to return to her career as a full-time writer. Her son was getting ready to go to college, and it was a time of transition for them as a family as well. Stacey was fortunate to find a buyer for the cafe and pass it along to a new owner.

Stacey shared several key factors that were integral to making the choices and transitions she made along the way. She also spoke with me about how she might offer advice to others considering similar moves in their lives.

 I think the most important thing is to really know yourself. I know people who could never do this, because the stability of their job is so important. I was at my job for thirty years, so I understand stability. If you don't love your job, but it pays well, you have great benefits, and you're OK with work not being fulfilling, then transitions could be really hard. If you say I don't care about the big house and nice cars, I'm OK if we have to change our lifestyle because this is more important, then the transition will be easier. That's what I found. I've grown more as a person and am less interested in material things.

The other thing about a transition is you take your skills with you. The interpersonal and research skills that I learned as a reporter, or any other skills that I had, I could take with me. So even though you're making a huge transition, you're still you, and you get to use those skills in your new work, in your new life.

Mark and Stacey's stories offer us scenarios of people who had various responsibilities, including raising children, while making significant career transitions to create more fulfilling work lives. While they both achieved their dreams, their journeys took many unexpected turns. This is clear: they were happy about the paths they took, satisfied with what they learned, and the decisions they made along the way.

Stacey remarked how her son had a front-row seat watching her work as a business owner with all its joys and challenges. I often discuss this idea with my clients. For many of us, the only role models or context we have for what it means to be a working person or have a career is the example that is set for us by our parents or other influential adults. We might choose careers that follow in their footsteps—or alternatively, choose to go in an opposite direction. Either way, the examples we witnessed during those formative years influenced our earliest impressions about careers and the world of work.

As we become working parents, how often do we pause and think about the messages we send our children about what it means to go to work every day or to make a living? When we tell them they can be anything they want to be, do they see by our example what could be possible? Most importantly, I am suggesting that we do our best to provide positive and proactive modeling for our children as we engage in our careers and work lives.

Don't worry that children never listen to you;
worry that they are always watching you.

—Robert Fulghum

Reflective Questions and Guiding Activities

Regardless of whether you are a working parent, most of us have responsibilities in our lives that compel us to hold fast to a secure paycheck or stable benefits which enable us to meet our obligations. As you answer the following questions consider the symbolism of the safety announcement made on every flight before it takes off: If the cabin pressure changes, an oxygen mask will appear. Put the mask on yourself first and then help others. How often are you putting everything and everyone else ahead of your own needs and happiness? To what degree are you truly helping them when you put yourself second or last, all the time?

Self-Assessment

On a scale of 1 (not ready now) to 10 (ready to go for it), how ready are you to embark on a career transition (new job or career reinvention) at this time in your life?

What does your score mean to you? Be as specific as possible in articulating your feelings and thoughts about what it means to you to engage in a career transition at this time.

If your chosen score was two to three points higher than your original score, what would your experience look like in terms of your thoughts, feelings, and activities related to pursuing your career transition?

What activities might you be considering or doing at that higher comfort level? What kinds of information, relationships, or opportunities would become available to you from that place?

What might get in the way or prevent you from elevating your score? Name as many concerns or obstacles that you can.

What actions can you take to raise your score in the next six months to one year? It may help to speak about your options with a trusted colleague, or friend to percolate a few ideas, or hire a coach to explore your options in more depth.

Here are some recommended approaches that have proven effective for a multitude of professionals:

Create Your Own Job Description(s)

Give yourself some time, many days to do this exercise. Make a list of all the 'jobs' you hold in your life (parent, spouse, volunteer, employee, boss, coach, friend, caretaker, child, etc.) and write a job description in detail for each role. Next to each task with the description, label them as an H (have-to) or a W (want-to). Be brutally honest with yourself. Ask yourself, is there anyone else who can perform these functions in my place? How often can someone else perform them? Can you completely eliminate anything from your job descriptions?

Now, after this exercise has had some time to marinate in your mind, revise the job descriptions into those that you really want create a new description that captures what you are desiring. Some of your current jobs may still need to be done by you, but by laying it all out you can see more clearly where you stand, what choices you may have and think about how you can proceed from here.

Hire a Coach

Working with a coach can help you to clarify the issues you are considering, weigh your options, and make decisions based on a reflective process, thus enabling you to make choices which are aligned with your values. In doing so, you will feel greater ownership of the decisions and go into the changes you make with a stronger focus and sense of purpose.

Consult with a Financial Professional or Wealth Advisor

Making a change that could affect your financial stability can be daunting, and if you have not already engaged the services or advice of a financial or wealth advisor, now may be the time to do so. There are a variety of licensed and certified financial professionals available, so it is important that you choose one who has a business model and approach with which you feel comfortable. A referral from a trusted friend or other professional, such as an accountant, may be your best way to identify a good advisor. Ultimately you want to find someone you can trust to give you an accurate picture of your current financial situation and to help you think about your future. Once you have a clearer view of this, you can then determine your level of risk tolerance for making decisions about employment.

Access Your Alumni Associations

Many colleges and universities have robust alumni programs that include networking events and other opportunities to connect with fellow alumni in a variety of focused and social settings. The chance to engage with other alumni who may also have numerous responsibilities that compete with their desire to make career shifts could provide fertile common ground for further conversation and support. Many alumni offices are organizing career events and offering career-oriented webinars, which builds relationships amongst alumni as well.

Suggested reading:

Reinventing You: Define Your Brand, Imagine Your Future[2] by Dorie Clark

Whether you want to advance faster at your present company, change jobs, or make the jump to a new field entirely, *Reinventing You* provides a step-by-step guide to help you assess your unique strengths, develop a compelling personal brand, and ensure that others recognize the powerful contribution you can make.

4

CAREERS ARE NOT FORMED IN A STRAIGHT LINE

If you don't like the road you are walking,
start paving another one.

—DOLLY PARTON

Many of us were raised to believe that a "life-well-lived" includes a linear succession of milestones and achievements. This begins with getting an education and leads to developing a profession or livelihood, while starting and raising a family. Ultimately, one is rewarded with a retirement that includes enjoying grandchildren and leisure activities.

We may have even thought our parents' path looked like this, until we were old enough to realize they were fallible human beings and life didn't really happen that way. What's really funny is that although we have come to understand that people are less than perfect and that life is full of off-ramps and potholes, deep inside we remain attached to a linear narrative—or model of what must occur to achieve a good, solid, and complete life. I have spoken with people from different cultures, generations, and socioeconomic back-grounds, and while my evidence is empirical, they all indicate that they grew up with expectations of a linear path to a fulfilling life. I am sure if we put them side-by-side, the scenarios would differ, and the age by which each person discovered that life truly was not linear would certainly vary. Yet there comes a time in most people's lives when they say to themselves one of these statements:

- *I assumed I would have reached specific benchmarks by this time in my life.*
- *I never could have predicted that things would have turned out in these ways.*
- *If I had known then what I know now, I would have...*
- *I thought I would have conquered these challenges by now.*
- *I did all the right things (followed the rules), and it didn't turn out as expected.*
- *It is amazing how things evolved!*

David Shriner-Cahn

My friend and colleague, David Shriner-Cahn, is a great example of this phenomenon as he reached a point in his life where he questioned his career choices. About five years into his professional life, David realized that his path would include some curves. Earning his master's degree in chemical engi-neering from Cornell in the 1970s came with very linear, somewhat predictable expectations, according to David.

 I went to grad school, then got thrown into the working world, where there really is no calendar progression like you have in school. I had a full-time job designing chemical plants, and I could have done that for probably forty-plus years? And I'm like, is this really what I want? The reality was, I wasn't crazy about the work I was doing. I was good at it, and I made a good living.

David left his first engineering job and joined a second company, although he was clear it would not be his life's work. Again, he was doing well, receiving affirmation from others, and earning a good living. A month after his second annual performance review, in which he got a raise, David was laid off. He was told that the company didn't have enough business to keep him busy. David wasn't totally shocked, as he had sensed that the company wasn't doing well.

David viewed his layoff as an opportunity to assess and reflect on his career. He spent more than a year in a combination of activities—including half-heartedly looking for engineering positions—but the economy wasn't great, so it became increasingly hard to find a job. During that time, David was guided towards a program called Life/Work Design: a process that includes self-discovery, goal setting, and strategic planning modules coupled with significant coaching support to help participants achieve tangible results.

As David dove into the program, he found it to be extremely effective. It helped him to gain clarity on what he most loved to do, what his competencies were, and who he wanted to serve. He said it was as if a lightbulb turned on inside him.

Two months after finishing the Life/Work Design program, David got a job in a completely different field in which he had no formal training. He went into the nonprofit sector, becoming the executive director of a synagogue. This was a job he would grow into and thrive within for twenty years.

Everyone closest to me thought I was crazy. I
believe it's because when people hear the kind of
change you're making, they self-reflect and think
about what they would do in a similar situation.
And often change makes people really uncomfortable.

While he did not have the same formal training as many
other executive directors, David explained that the role was
actually a natural fit for him. He had the skills that the role
required from prior paid roles, but as he explained, "It just
wasn't linear. And to the bystanders, it wasn't particularly
logical."

After twenty years at the synagogue, David felt he had
reached a professional plateau. He wanted to be an
entrepreneur to have more control over what he was doing, so
he leveraged the relationships and experience he had built
over the years to start a nonprofit management consulting
practice. The business evolved into a mixture of nonprofit and
small-business clients. Over the years, he began working more
with solopreneurs who were consultants, coaches, selling their
knowledge or creative services.

David provides coaching and consulting to his clients on
how to run their businesses, including establishing healthy
revenue models and sales/marketing strategies and how to
stay profitable while solving their client's most complex problems. He helps his clients to see paths to more efficient
revenue-generating options, while also thinking strategically
about sales and marketing.

In 2014, David started a podcast called *Smashing the Plateau*,
featuring the tagline, "Helps you get unstuck—so you can do
what you love and get paid what you're worth." Podcasting
was a new content creation territory at that time. While he
smashed his own plateau in 2006 by leaving full-time employment and becoming an entrepreneur, David wanted to estab-

lish a new place where people could know him as a thought leader. The podcast also changed the way he did business, in that he was able to meet many new people, form partnerships on projects, and expand his practice into new areas.

 You want to have a place where people can get to know you, because people will buy from those people they know, like, and trust. One way for people to get to know you is by creating content. People write books, blogs, do videos and have YouTube channels. I like meeting new people and asking questions. For me, a podcast works pretty well.

In 2019, David created a second podcast, called *Going Solo*. He saw the critical need for content that addressed "the trauma of late-career job loss and what it's like to go from being highly skilled and well-compensated to unemployment, how to deal with it, and how to reinvent yourself as an entrepreneur, satisfying your soul and supporting your life-style." David features individuals who have survived and succeeded in those circumstances as well as interviews with experts who offer advice to listeners considering their own transitions from job loss to entrepreneurship.

David's podcasts showcase two contrasting viewpoints about how careers rarely follow a linear path. We hear stories of people who took charge of their careers and made transitions with *Smashing the Plateau*. *Going Solo* begins with events that the individual had not planned on, then eventually leads to steps to entrepreneurship. Looking through either lens, we see that once people take charge of their professional lives, they can consider the options and make choices along the squiggly pathways that most of us typically travel during our careers.

The trajectory of David's less-than-linear career path is instructive for anyone feeling stuck, lost, or frustrated. He points to some key decisions and actions that significantly inspired and supported his growth over his many transitions.

> One really important transition I made was from engineering to the nonprofit sector. I spent a year trying to figure things out on my own. Then I joined a group program, and two months later, I had a job. One thing I recommend that people do—and no matter where they are career-wise, as an employee or entrepreneur—join a group with people who are struggling with similar issues, like frustration, fear, discomfort, etc. You will hear experiences that others have gone through that you can learn from.

David found the Life/Work Design program so effective that he uses the process today with his current business clients. As an entrepreneur, he continues to engage in professional mastermind and other partnerships that fuel his work. His podcasts and consulting work have been featured in high-profile publications such as *Forbes* and *Inc.* magazines.

> Life is not linear. Success is not linear. And there are a lot of twists and turns. You need to recognize that and be open to change, trying paths that you may be a little unsure about. Frankly, when we step outside of our comfort zone, that's when we grow the most.

Mac Prichard

When Mac Prichard graduated from college, there were three things he knew he wanted to do: get paid to write, do human rights advocacy, and work in politics. He admits he could not have articulated them as succinctly at the time, yet he has done them all during his career, in addition to many other jobs. Along the way, Mac made some big professional transitions, and he learned a lot along the way.

Mac grew up in eastern Iowa. He attended the University of Iowa, earning a bachelor's degree in political science with a minor in Latin American studies.

 Growing up in Iowa, you get the political bug. Because of the caucuses, presidential candidates come through every four years, so I used to skip high school to check out candidates. My mother was involved in politics and was on the bargaining team for her local union. Service and involvement in the community were important values in my family. That inspired my college studies.

After graduation, Mac worked in Iowa for six months on a US Senate campaign. He then moved to Washington, DC to work for a human rights organization, where he learned public affairs skills, how to talk to reporters, how to write, and how to engage legislative staff on Capitol Hill. Two years later, he was referred to a job in Boston with the Unitarian Universalist Service Committee, another human rights organization. In that role, he took members of Congress on fact-finding trips to Central America during a period of great unrest and violence, including civil wars and a revolution.

 I thought job hunting in my twenties was easy, because I had three great jobs right out of the gate. Immediately after graduating from the University of Iowa, I worked on a US Senate race, a job I found through a classified ad. Then I went to Washington, DC, to work for an organization where I'd had an undergraduate internship, so they knew me and offered me a position. I then found the position in Boston through a referral. What I didn't understand at the time was how important it was to set clear goals when you were considering making a change in your focus.

After four years, Mac left his job at the Unitarian Universalist Service Committee under the assumption that it would be simple to find a new role. This was in the mid-1980s, a time when people would consider leaving a job without another one lined up. Mac headed into a period of struggle, because he wasn't clear about his goals. He did what most job seekers would do at that time: every Sunday, he'd get the *Boston Globe*, open it up to the classified ads, and circle five or six jobs that he thought were either interesting or that he was qualified for. Then he'd send off his generic resumes by mail on Sunday or Monday. Occasionally, he would get responses, and even interviews, but he never got an offer.

> Once I got into the interview room, it was clear that, to the interviewer, I didn't know what I wanted. And when you're unclear about your goals, that's a challenge, because you're competing against candidates who know what they want to do, so they're going to be very confident, focused, and more successful in the interviews.

That was a painful yet eye-opening lesson for Mac to learn in his mid-twenties. As he struggled with what to do next, he volunteered on the issues team for the congressional campaign of Joe Kennedy II, son of Robert F. Kennedy. Once the election was over, Mac still felt stuck and wasn't sure where he wanted to go next. Fortunately, his wife worked at a local university and introduced him to a colleague in career services on campus. Mac had one conversation with her and gained enough insight to determine that he wanted to work in media relations within government or politics, yet he also realized that he needed more information.

Mac knew that he needed to have conversations with people who were well-connected and could refer him to the types of roles he was seeking. He started by identifying and contacting people who were doing communications and media relations work in state and local government. Mac inquired about potential opportunities and how he could best position himself as a candidate and apply his transferable skills.

Two months later in one of those networking conversations, Mac learned about a communications position that was not yet posted with Boston's Big Dig, a multi-billion-dollar mega-project rerouting an interstate highway through the heart of the city, turning it into a 1.5-mile tunnel. Mac applied, competing for the job against other candidates who were also referred for the role, and was offered the job. The position was never publicly posted. This is a great example of finding work through the hidden job market.

This was a significant career change for Mac, as he went from the world of human rights advocacy and US Latin American policy to issues work for a congressional race—and then on to state and local government. He found the role at the Big Dig by remaining open-minded to learning all he could about his new arena of work interest. While he did have the referral that helped him get the interview, it wasn't offered due to a political connection or personal favor. Mac initially presented himself through networking as a focused person who knew what he wanted, and by doing so, his contact was well informed and therefore willing to make the referral.

The job with Boston's Big Dig led Mac to another position in state government two years later, where he served as the spokesperson for a state agency that resettled refugees in

Massachusetts. During the two years he worked in that role, Mac realized that many of his colleagues were advancing their careers and saw that the field was competitive. He believed that in order to grow and compete for higher-level jobs, he needed to have additional credentials, so he applied to and attended the John F. Kennedy School of Government at Harvard University where he earned his master's degree in public administration. Once Mac finished his degree, he and his wife decided that it would be nice to live in a new city. They chose Portland, Oregon, due to its reputation for having a good quality of life. It was intended to be a five-year plan, but it turned out to be so enjoyable that they stayed and raised their family there.

Mac's first job in Portland was as the communications director for a mayoral candidate, and that led to other positions in city government in the state capital of Salem. He did experience a nine-month period of unemployment due to budget cuts, and in retrospect was disappointed that he did not spend the time as productively as he had when he was out of work in Boston.

 I regret not volunteering after I left City Hall back then. I didn't volunteer, because my pride got the better of me. With more than ten years of professional experience and a graduate degree from Harvard, I told myself I should get paid for my work. That was a big mistake, because I sat at home when I could have been helping others, improving my skills, and growing my network. I had nothing to show for those months.

Mac managed to bounce back, becoming the communications director for the Oregon Employment Department, and that led to work as a spokesman for several state agencies. He then became a speechwriter for the governor, and later transitioned to communications work in the non-profit sector.

In 2007, Mac started his own public relations company, Prichard Communications, that serves foundations, non-profits, and government agencies. Over the years, through two significant periods of unemployment and many rewarding years developing his career, he learned the vital importance of networking. According to Mac, networking is about being of service to others. And one of the ways he did that was by sharing job postings. So, when he left the state government, Mac started sharing the occasional job posting that came across his desk with former colleagues who he wanted to stay in touch with.

 Being out of work for two long periods taught me the importance of learning job-hunting skills, staying in touch with people, and serving my professional network. Mac's List began as a simple series of forwarded job postings to professional colleagues I wanted to help and remain in contact with. Today, it's a six-figure business with a staff of four that serves tens of thousands of readers. Service to others remains central to our business and our mission. It's a value I recommend everyone make part of their career.

After almost ten years, Mac's List grew by word of mouth to a list of 4,000 people who were receiving job postings. At that point, Mac had to start charging to manage the listings. Today, Mac's List is a regional job board that publishes about 700 job postings a month to help people find fulfilling work and help employers find talented workers in Oregon and Washington. What distinguishes Mac's List from other job boards is its commitment to community service, teaching job seekers how to skillfully look for work, and assisting employers in improving hiring practices. For job seekers and employers, Mac's List provides a lot of content on their website about how to strengthen job hunting as a skill and how to get better at hiring.

 I've had a lot of stressful jobs, and you never quite shake off the job when you go home, whether you're a solopreneur, or you're running a small business with a number of employees as I do. I'm comfortable with that kind of stress. Because of the opportunities I've had, I've learned how to manage it. I would say the choices I've made, when you look at all the different jobs I've had, there is a common denominator that runs through them all which is wanting to make a difference about issues I care about in the community where I live and work.

Both David's and Mac's stories offer us clear examples of how careers can take multiple turns instead of that straight-line path that many of us expected to follow as our lifetime identity. Yet, there are logical explanations for why many of us grew up with these assumptions and expectations.

As a member of the baby boomer generation, David Shriner-Cahn said it well:

It's like leaving the comfort zone of being uncomfortable. There are many people out there working a job, being an engineer, for example, because it's a respectable career and it pays well enough. Why would you leave something steady and solid like that? The goal of being happy in some generations was a lower priority, especially for those who lived during the Depression, where people were content just to have food on the table. It's hard to imagine under those conditions that somebody would change careers or take a risk like that.

Those in the baby boomer or Gen X generations received strong messages about the importance of a college education or having a trade that would lead to better employment options and higher salaries. Many of us had role models who either followed that straightforward route or struggled to achieve that kind of stable, solid employment trajectory. Some employers had mandatory retirement ages and company pension plans. These programs were more common in the US, while there is a great deal of evidence showing that most adults have had at least two careers in their lifetimes. Today, the number of occupations a person has during their life could easily be much higher. Yet many still retain these expectations of a linear path "I will be this kind of professional working person" for the better part of my adult life until I retire; after that, my life will be very different. It makes complete sense that this message has consistently traveled through the generations, as most people have had no other models demonstrated for them.

Younger generations may have also been raised with similar expectations, as their parents and grandparents were boomers and Gen Xers. Yet, we know the outlook for the future of work has shifted significantly. We need to be far better prepared to navigate the fluctuations in the marketplace that could substantially impact our professional lives. I recommend that people have a Plan B (a backup plan) and Plan C (a way to raise some cash plan) if their employment situation changes unexpectedly and they need to keep paying the bills.

Ultimately, I suggest that we think like entrepreneurs in our careers as we drive our professional direction. The era when employers would offer the kind of benefits that take care of their employees over the long haul is essentially gone. Change is the only constant, and we need to be prepared to adapt.

The first step is to notice the expectations and assumptions you have had about where you think your career is going—and stay open, curious, and alert to where you want it to go. Don't just look in front of you or up the ladder. Look sideways, underneath, behind, and all over. You are the driver!

————————

In almost every case, nothing is stopping you, nothing is holding you back but your own thoughts about yourself and about 'how life is.'

—NEALE DONALD WALSCH

Reflective Questions and Guiding Activities

As you answer the following questions, pay attention to your pace. While these questions appear similar to those in previous chapters, they are framed differently. Slow down to notice how your assumptions and expectations have shaped the path of your career. What guided your decisions at each intersection of your career? Can you recall the source of the choices you made and how you felt about the directions you pursued? This is not about labeling anything right or wrong but rather understanding the foundations for your pivot points and how they served your purposes at the time.

Self-Assessment

On a scale of 1 (not comfortable) to 10 (very comfortable), how comfortable are you with pursuing a career transition (new job or career reinvention) without knowing where it will land?

What does your score mean to you? Be as specific as possible in articulating your feelings, thoughts, and questions about what it means to you to engage in a career transition at this time.

If your chosen score was two to three points higher than your original score, what would your experience look like in terms of your thoughts, feelings, and activities related to pursuing your career transition?

What activities might you be considering or doing at that higher comfort level? What kinds of information, relationships, or opportunities would become available to you from that place?

What might get in the way or prevent you from elevating your score? Create a list of as many concerns or obstacles as you can imagine.

What actions can you take to raise your score in the next six months to one year? It may help to speak about your options with a trusted colleague, or friend to percolate a few ideas, or hire a coach to explore your options in more depth.

Here are some suggested activities that you can try to move your professional journey forward:

Do an Adult Internship or Shadow a Professional on the Job

Adult internships have become more popular as people are eager to learn new skills and experience different work environments. Programs exist on the community level and some people create their own internship or shadowing experiences through their networks. See the resources section for a few places to begin your search.

Listen to Podcasts

Podcasts are an excellent resource for obtaining current information, real life stories, and a wide variety of perspectives on any topic of interest. In the career arena, there are so many podcasts available to listen to and learn from that it may be difficult to identify which ones are offering you solid information. Of course, I can recommend my weekly podcast, Work from the Inside Out, which features stories of career transitions that inspire and inform. A great resource for narrowing down your options was created by Mac Prichard, who is profiled in this chapter. Since 2017, Mac has curated his annual *Top Career Podcasts Guide*, a single source for the best podcast shows dedicated to helping professionals look for work and grow their careers. Additionally, Mac hosts an excellent podcast, Find Your Dream Job.

5

DON'T DEFAULT TO WHAT YOU'RE GOOD AT

Sometimes, in life and in love, risks must be taken.
One never knows what may happen.

—MOIRA ROSE

As a child or teenager, did any influential adults in your life tell you how well you did something, suggesting that you pursue a particular or related profession? They meant well and were encouraging you with their well-intentioned guidance. You agreed with them and welcomed their support. Then you grew up and developed those strengths to become a happy, talented professional. Wonderful! That's one scenario.

Perhaps those well-intentioned adults were right about your strengths, but you were not sure that you wanted to pursue those disciplines as fully as they thought you should. Still, you listened to them. You developed a career in that area, elevating your position to the point where you became well established over many years. Eventually, you realized that you never really enjoyed it, even though you were good at it.

Now you feel stuck. You have reached a standard of living that you have become accustomed to; people are counting on you, bills to pay, and besides that, what else could you possibly do? Rest assured, you are not alone.

Simply put, we can be good or talented at something that we do not enjoy (for me, it is toilet cleaning). Therefore, it is essential to check in with ourselves and acknowledge what we like to do. Chances are pretty good that if we enjoy a skill or activity, we will probably be good at it. For some people, discovering what you enjoy can be dramatic and may launch a complete career change or a minor shift in one's work.

For most of us, our context for work or a professional life starts from the models we had during our formative years. My parents enjoyed long careers, each in a single profession for decades, while other people had different examples of what it meant to go to work or have a job. Those images were ingrained in us and influenced how we pursued our own professional identities. Some of us may have created expectations to follow in our parents' footsteps, while others felt compelled to find a different path. We may have believed we were groomed for something particular ("you are so good in science, you should be a doctor") or feel that we had little to no guidance or direction. Then there was the generic "you can be anything you want to be" encouragement, which left some of us feeling loved and nurtured—and others feeling lost.

Corey Blake

Corey Blake started his career as an actor in Los Angeles. Like many people who began there, LA is not where he ended up. The difference between Corey and most acting hopefuls is that he was actually "making it" when he decided to move his life in other directions. But before we jump ahead, let's first take a couple of steps back to where he started.

Corey attended college, earning a degree in theater arts and studying acting from the stage. A year after graduation, he moved to Los Angeles and spent the next three years doing what most people do there. He worked other jobs to survive, using whatever available income he could to support his career—getting better headshots, taking acting classes, and going to showcases. In 1998, Corey got his first break. He saw that 20th Century Fox was casting for a film called *Fight Club*. Corey decided to write a very heartfelt letter to the casting director, expressing his passion for acting and that he needed someone to give him a chance so that he could get into the actor's union to gain more opportunities. As a result of that letter, Corey got to work eight days on *Fight Club* as a Screen Actor's Guild background actor. Shortly thereafter and on the same day, he booked a Mountain Dew commercial and a guest role on the popular TV show *Sabrina the Teenage Witch*. When it rains, it pours!

Corey's Mountain Dew spot aired for the first time during the 2000 Super Bowl and was named one of the fifty greatest Super Bowl commercials of all time. He was cast in commercials for Hasbro, Wrigley's, American Express, Pepsi, and Miller beer as well as a few feature films. He also guest-starred on popular television shows like *Buffy the Vampire Slayer* and *The Shield*. The acting was fun at times, but he "always felt like a crayon in other people's crayon box."

 At this point, I'm in my mid-twenties, and getting cast for acting jobs, but I'm a tool for other people. There was never a feeling of belonging, because I would show up for one to five days, essentially coming into someone else's family, like a guest. The core of the production had been there for months or a year. I came and left. I started producing and directing, because I needed to be more involved in the creative process.

While his acting career was successful, Corey felt purposeless. He didn't believe he was put on this earth to encourage kids to drink Mountain Dew and stuff cheeseburgers down their throats. He wanted a greater sense of control in his work. Between 1999 and 2003, he started two storytelling companies. He brought together a group of actors and a professional crew to shoot the first film he would produce. That led to a second film—which he directed—and then a third and a fourth film.

At the same time, Corey was developing leadership skills, such as how to inspire people and manage complex projects. He did a lot right but still made some huge mistakes that, as he tells it, eroded people's trust in him and, ultimately, blew up both of those companies. Those lessons were excruciatingly painful, yet they would also prove vital down the road, as Corey searched for a healthier way to lead and began seeing a better way to do things.

As Corey approached his late twenties, he was driving to a commercial audition and grumbling about needing to step away from producing and directing. Suddenly, he realized that some younger kid would kill for the regular audition opportunities that he was receiving. Since he was so irritated about feeling pulled away from his other artistic endeavors, maybe it was time to make room for others who wanted those opportunities, he thought. When Corey made that decision, however, he didn't expect to find himself in a full-blown identity crisis.

 If I wasn't an actor, who I was? It was a challenging dichotomy: how does success appear on the outside, versus what does it feel like inside? Mountain Dew, Pepsi, Miller beer, and Wrigley's gum are recognized brands. That left me feeling accomplished, but they used my talent to emotionally open people up to buy their product. At times I was aligned and felt like I was contributing to products or services that were beneficial, but more often, I wasn't. I was paid well, which can be confusing. Commercials, especially, could feel like winning at the slots. Everyone near me was saying, "You're doing what we are all out here to do." So, I'm getting cheered on, certainly by my mother, who loved having a son on TV she could talk about. Eventually, I had to come to terms with the reality that I wasn't fulfilled by this work.

This was a highly transformative time for Corey, as he was also getting married and moving back to his hometown of Chicago. He affectionately refers to this period as his "three-year temper tantrum" in which he needed to figure out who he was and how to make meaning of his work. While still in LA, Corey started his third company, the Round Table Companies (RTC), which he took it with him to Chicago. While he was finding his way into work that felt meaningful, he was still at the bottom of a new ladder.

Corey credits some strong personal development work with multiple therapists and coaches as instrumental to improving his self-awareness and helping him articulate his goals. At the same time, he was also learning to be married. Upon reflection, Corey wonders if he needed to struggle to the degree that he did, yet his journey to self-discovery had some nuance to it.

Corey spent solid time on a successful path, one that many people fail in. And a lot of people were telling him how good he was at it, yet he was wrestling within himself: *this isn't it for me, or is it, maybe it is, but I don't know what IT is?*

 I'm a collider; I know who I am by how I press up against the world and by how it pushes back. We each have different styles for self-discovery. For me, that three-year period was a huge struggle. In LA, there's a lot to press up against, so I was able to define myself more easily. When I wasn't an actor anymore, it was like decision paralysis. After I moved back home, I didn't have things to collide with regularly so I didn't know how to define myself and didn't have a robust emotional toolkit to manage my struggling.

Initially, Corey's current company, RTC, was a purely transactional business. Searches on Craigslist revealed all of these businesspeople who needed writers, and all of these writers who were looking for jobs; neither seemed to understand how to communicate with the other. That communication felt relatively comfortable to Corey. But rather than being just an agent and bringing businesspeople and writers together, he remained part of the process and helped both sides to exceed their expectations of what was possible. It became a growing business where he could continually replace himself by bringing other people onboard. Through his history in LA, Corey started attracting some world-class coaches and CEOs who wanted to tell their stories or share their experiences leading other people, and he quickly found himself addicted to creating books.

I love the story that Corey tells about one of the first books his company published. His client was a CEO who, in his younger years, had been a gang member and drug dealer who was a high school drop out. He wanted to give back to Latino kids and inspire them to see a different way forward, as he had done when he got his GED, served in the military, and then entered the workforce—eventually rising to be the VP of a publicly-traded company before growing a world-class company of his own. When teachers started using the book, Corey helped his client develop a curriculum, followed by a comic book to reach younger kids—and then a coloring book to reach an even younger population. To date, those books have reached tens of thousands of students.

Many of the books landed in the hands of existing gang members who were inspired and curious to consider leaving that life. If they were caught by their gang leaders with the books, they would be penalized with negative points known as demerits. Needless to say, Corey found this kind of work far more fulfilling than acting. Now, that's a great example of *work from the inside out.*

Corey pursued more work with authors and publishing projects, as he wanted to collaborate in creating transformative experiences for people and groups. Over the years, Corey's leadership and vision for RTC has expanded its relationship with storytellers and authors by offering a broader menu of services to support authors, business leaders, and other thought leaders in putting their voices out into the world. They use a team approach to creativity and partner with clients based on their needs and desires. For authors writing a book, the process may include manuscript development, book writing coaching, manuscript analysis, editing, illustration, packaging, publishing, and book launch.

As RTC was growing and had a solid team in place, Corey began to think about the next steps.

 I had my head down in RTC for eight years when I was invited to the Conscious Capitalism CEO Summit, which at that time included 250 CEOs of companies $5m+ committed to business that elevates humanity. I was questioning, 'What am I doing here?' By the end, I knew exactly why I was there. I had a strong compulsion to serve that community. They had invested a lot in their intellectual capacity and loved this consciousness concept. Yet bringing conscious behavior to business is not necessarily intuitive, and that's the world I came from.

After the conference, Corey reflected on an insight and then shared it with his team. He noticed that in conference spaces, people didn't seem to get comfortable until it was time to leave, and he felt that if they were not comfortable, they were not taking risks. Corey believed this pointed to a lot of lost opportunities. RTC, being good at creating human experiences, compelled him to prompt his team with some questions to explore how they might meet this need:

- How can we expedite the ability for people to stop the mental chatter of *how am I better or worse?*
- Or *who's more successful than me?*
- How can we quiet the mind and highlight to everyone the ways in which we are all the same?

From there, Corey and the RTC team created what they lovingly call *The Vulnerability Wall*—an art installation that asks event participants to fill out anonymous responses to a question being posed to them. Then RTC artists turn their words into art—live, during the course of that event. These wall installations have made a deep impact on the culture and connections across conferences and companies like Microsoft, ADP, and Workday—with lasting effects.

Corey and his team took their creative process from writing and publishing books and hosting vulnerability walls, to working with businesses to tell their stories and build their brands using authentic and vulnerable storytelling. They added event experiences, and documentary and animated films to their slate of offerings, to showcase a client company's vision and branding. Installing a vulnerability wall or creating a book or film can be an expensive and large endeavor, so they also created a lower-cost card game, *Vulnerability is*

Sexy™, in order to offer that connective experience to more people.

 We started as a book company, and now we have evolved to solving complex business challenges with various forms of storytelling. We go into bigger organizations to do culture work, which is all about their internal storytelling. Whether we are supporting internal or external brand amplification, we do so by zeroing in on the authentic human components of the people who power the brand, and then we express those through stories that create gravitational pull around the business. We have been blessed to attract remarkable and courageous leaders who want to serve the world. And we're having a blast.

Rachel Rice

Rachel Rice contacted me several years ago as she was connecting with professionals operating private practices in our region. She was in the process of establishing a new business and wanted to learn as much as she could about running a successful practice. Rachel knew enough to know what she didn't know, and it showed in her laser-focused, yet humble manner. I quickly became enchanted with her as she tuned in, asking me great questions; on top of that, I found her story to be enormously intriguing. Shortly thereafter, I signed on with her as a client. Later, she helped me to make the decision to launch my podcast and became my first podcast guest.

Rachel is the founder and CEO of Five Rhythms Consulting, a corporate executive turned peak performance consultant who works with individuals to reach their full potential by aligning their energy to their purpose. She is a certified Eden Energy Medicine practitioner, authorized energy medicine teacher, a Reiki Master, and a meditations leader. Prior to opening Five Rhythms Consulting, Rachel spent most of her career in corporate leadership roles, most recently as the chief marketing officer for New York Life Retirement Plan Services, where she oversaw marketing, product development, web strategy, and creative execution. What makes Rachel unique today is the way she integrates energy medicine and energy psychology techniques into her work and leadership style— with the goal of driving the best possible outcomes for the individuals and organizations she serves.

 When I was in corporate, I wanted to be the best possible version of myself, all of the time. I put a lot of pressure on myself to perform to be the best at what I was doing to serve the organization. And I was looking for any tool that would help me to do that. Starting in my twenties, I learned how to meditate. I started studying yoga, I was physically fit, I tried to eat really healthy food. I was doing all these things to take the best care of my mind and body. I discovered that those things just weren't enough given the environment I was in, and the level of responsibility that I had. I wasn't sleeping well. I felt stressed most of the time.

Then, somebody gave Rachel a book about energy medicine. She was very skeptical about it, but periodically, she would open the book, read something, and try some of the techniques. Rachel was surprised when she realized that she could feel the energy move in her body. For several years, she would occasionally pick up the book and try something new. She noticed the shifts in her energy and how her thinking would feel more organized.

There was another factor that played a role in her skepticism about the scope or reach of this energy stuff. For most of her life, Rachel had been what is known as a "highly sensitive" person (HSP). An HSP is someone who experiences acute physical, mental, or emotional responses to stimuli. While we all may experience things this way at times, HSPs consistently have these kinds of responses. Rachel has always been sensitive to her own and other people's feelings, the environment, foods, and smells. For her, it's been considered more of a liability than something that was helping her, except for when she was in tune with other people.

With the energy medicine book, she would open it, try something out that was meant to help her be more present or organized in her thinking, and she could feel the energy moving in her body and would feel better. While preparing for an important meeting or a presentation, she began accessing this new toolkit, finding that it put her in the best state of mind and body to deliver her message. So she started relying on these tools more. But then she began to wonder if it was her highly sensitive nature that enabled her to use these tools effectively, or could these be helpful to other people?

Rachel started sharing the energy techniques with people in her work environment. As chief marketing officer, she invited them to a lunch-and-learn session explaining, "I want to share some tools I'm using. They're different than what we might ordinarily expect in a corporate environment, but I'm using them myself. As a leader in the organization, I wanted to share what I have been using to help you." She started with a pre-survey before teaching them the techniques, which constituted a five-minute routine. Then Rachel asked them a series of questions about vitality skills on a five-point scale, such as:

- *How are you feeling today?*
- *What is your energy level?*
- *How well are you communicating your creativity with people?*

She met with whoever wanted to come every day for five minutes, and they did the same five-minute routine. At the end of thirty days, Rachel surveyed them again. For the group that took the pre- and post-survey, she saw a 20 percent lift in their overall vitality skill scores. It was enough for Rachel to see this little five-minute energy routine was really having a positive impact. People shared with her that they no longer got their three o'clock slump; they felt more vibrant, more creative, engaged; and their relationships were better.

Rachel had always had an interest in alternative care and methods, but there was something extraordinary about energy medicine. Rachel decided to enroll in the two-year Eden Energy Medicine Practitioner Certification program, while she remained in her corporate job.

 Then, I had a moment of truth. We were selling our company to an acquiring organization. As part of the senior leadership team, nine of us had to present to the acquiring organization. We spent months preparing and had several dry runs before the final day. During one dry run, one of my colleagues froze. He lost access to his words, to his body. His face went pale, and he stopped moving his hands. He took twice as long as he really had to deliver his message. It was painful for the rest of us to sit through that watching him struggle. And they moved him from first to last in the queue. That afternoon, I thought to myself, if this is how it's going to go on the final day, we're not going to sell the organization, which means that we'll need to go through another very painful process.

That afternoon, Rachel approached her colleague and offered to help him in any way he wanted. He had not attended her thirty-day, five-minute routine sessions—nor would she have expected him to as he was a more conservative person. Rachel told him that she had been using some different skills and techniques that were helping her to prepare and that she would be happy to share them if he was open to it. He was willing to try almost anything. Rachel taught him the techniques, and he reported that he immediately felt them in his body. She saw the color return to his face, the light come back to his eyes, and he was able to access his words. He remained calm and organized. On the final day, he aced his presentation. For Rachel, this was so much more than just helping out a colleague. It confirmed for her that these skills and techniques could be effective with a wide variety of individuals. This was a big pivot point for Rachel.

 Financial services is a very conservative culture, as everything is strictly regulated. I think my willingness to bring myself fully as I was into the workplace was challenging, because I had a corporate identity. I felt like accessing this other stuff might impact people's perception of me. And it did. There was some dismissiveness, condescension, or commentary about "what is that New Age thing?" I did a lot of internal work on myself around ego, who am I? What am I meant to be doing in this world? Am I really fully doing that in this role? I was always a hard worker putting in sixty, seventy, eighty hours at a time, and I was discovering that I wanted a higher return on my own investment, not just a higher return for an organization or an increase in compensation.

While the company was being acquired, Rachel had the opportunity to be considered for the presidency of the organization. She went home and talked to her husband about it. They discussed whether or not it was really what she wanted. He asked her if she wanted that additional level of responsibility and stress. She quickly realized the answer was no, as she was far more interested in the topic of energy.

Rachel hired a life coach who asked her some illuminating yet simple questions such as, "Who are you?" During their process, they identified what Rachel's ideal work could be and developed a plan to move in that direction. She knew she wanted to start her own business and was clear that she needed to move slowly, one small step at a time toward that shift. As a matter of practicality, Rachel had been the primary earner in her family, and their plan was for her to continue that role.

There were many questions to be answered, so Rachel crafted a business plan that included a few scenarios to ensure she had all her bases covered, including enough savings for her family to live on while she got the business started. Simultaneously, Rachel discussed her plans, estimates, and calculations with her husband to be sure that he was on board with everything. These were "we" conversations that had to be clear and affirmed in order for her to take the next steps.

 When people make a significant change, there are many things going on. I would call it a ping pong match, as there's this back and forth between fear and faith, trust, and love. Whenever I fell back into fear, I would slow down. It didn't matter how much effort I put in. I got in my own way. And whenever I fell more toward faith, trust, and possibility, I opened up. It was like putting your foot on the gas and the brake pedal, alternately. Somebody pointed it out to me, and I thought, I need to use the skills I teach my clients! I leveraged energy medicine. Holding my own neurovascular points on my head while thinking about these fears, I cleared them so that I could put effort into creating, building, and empowering people—and less on the fear about what might or might not happen.

In 2015, Rachel launched her business, Five Rhythms Consulting. Within a year and a half, she was seeing clients on a regular basis, getting referrals through word-of-mouth, and speaking in a variety of venues. That was a turning point. She renovated space in her home and took the business to the next level by partnering with a few colleagues to deliver training in organizations. They work with mid- to large-sized organizations that are interested in improving their leadership presence and communication capacities so that they can bring out the best in their people. Rachel feels that moving in the direction of energy medicine work has brought out the best in her and the lives of the people she serves.

 I believe that we each have a unique gift to bring to the world. And when we're not doing that, we're keeping that from others and from ourselves. Identify those gifts, invest in yourself, trust yourself, and continue to lean toward that direction. Even if it's baby steps, make those investments, work hard, and work smart. But work toward that direction of your natural, inherent gifts, and trust that they are yours. They're a gift to the world.

Both Rachel's and Corey's stories offer solid examples of people who excelled at their jobs. They were well compensated and had significant opportunities to grow, yet neither of them were feeling an internal connection or purpose behind what they were doing. We also saw how they each discovered the difference between being good at their jobs versus being who they truly wanted to be at work.

Corey's ability to open people up emotionally, allowing them to connect to their purpose and be their own best story-tellers, has become his life's work in its many iterations. Rachel's corporate-self evolved into an energy healer who is tuned in to help not only individuals but to speak powerfully to groups, helping them to experience themselves in ways that could propel them to a new level of success.

———

The curious paradox is that when I accept myself exactly as I am, then I can change.

—CARL ROGERS

Reflective Questions and Guiding Activities

While distinguishing your strengths from your preferences, which can overlap, answer the following questions. Over the course of your career, what choices have you made in terms of capitalizing on your strengths or following your desires? What influences played a role in those decisions and how did your choices change over time? ... or did they? What would you do differently as you go forward?

Self-Assessment

On a scale of 1 (completely unfulfilled) to 10 (deeply fulfilled), how fulfilled are you by the career path you are on today?

What does your score mean to you? Be as specific as possible in outlining your feelings and thoughts about where you believe you are on your current career path.

Assuming your score is two to three points higher, what would your career path or day-to-day work look like? How would you be spending your time? How would it feel on most days? What types of activities do you imagine yourself being engaged in?

What kinds of information, relationships, or opportunities would you imagine are available to you at this higher score?

What might get in the way or prevent you from elevating your score? Name as many concerns or obstacles as you can identify.

What actions can you take to raise your score in the next six months to one year? It may help to speak about your options with a trusted colleague or friend to spark a few ideas, or hire a coach to explore your options in more depth.

Here are some suggested activities that you can try to move your professional journey forward:

Know Yourself, Own Your Impact

When people begin to consider a career change, they usually have more clarity about what they don't want to do than what they would like to do. This can be distressing and cause some analysis paralysis, aka that stuck feeling. A great first step to getting unstuck is to think about times when people have thanked you for something you have done, and their appreciation "made your day." How do they describe the value or benefit you offered? Are the talents or behaviors they recognized you for attributes that you are proud of? How do those characteristics that distinguish you from others demonstrate the unique contributions you make as a leader, on a team, or with a client? Looking beyond your competency in those areas or skills that people have commended you for, do you derive genuine pleasure when you perform them? If so, how would you characterize them as your "special sauce"? Might there be a good metaphor to describe you or have people attached a term of endearment or nickname for your special contributions? In addition to reflecting on this, ask people who know you well or have worked with you to share their impressions of your impact in the workplace or other situations. Let it marinate, and seek further help if you need to wordsmith a good summary statement that captures your unique professional characteristics and contributions.

Ditch the Pitch—Create Your Branding Statement

Let's face it. No one talks in elevators and besides that, a well-rehearsed elevator pitch is delivered in such a humdrum manner that no one is really listening anyway. I recommend that you craft a personal branding statement which does not need to be memorized because it is a statement that will appear within the summary on your resume or LinkedIn profile. The ideas expressed in the statement can be expanded and used as key talking points to respond to inquiries such as, "Tell me about yourself." There are three essential components within a branding statement that can be garnered by answering the following questions:

- What role do you want?
- What single problem can you solve better than anyone else?
- How can you deliver value for your organization or client?

Here are examples of branding statements:

Digital Marketer: I develop powerful digital marketing strategies that help businesses attract new customers.

Operations Consultant: I help manufacturing companies improve their processes to reduce waste, get product to the customer faster, and increase profitability.

6

SUCCESS IS NOT A DESTINATION

Strive not to be a success, but rather to be of value.

—ALBERT EINSTEIN

How do you define success? Has it influenced the choices you have made in your professional and personal life? For many of us, the beliefs we have developed about what it means to be successful can steer the priorities we set in every aspect of our work and personal lives. Societal influences and what we learned during our formative years set the context for those beliefs, resulting in whether we feel compelled to follow the status quo or turn in a different direction. Most often, people define success in financial or material terms and through other benchmarks such as a succession of awards, promotions, and professional or personal affiliations.

The values, assumptions, and expectations we have held and aspired to have often become the guidelines by which we measure our self-esteem and define our identity. What is most important here, in my view, are not the specific data points we refer to as success, but rather how we feel about ourselves, our accomplishments, and the impact they have on those around us and beyond.

Several factors comprise what most people refer to as success. While we may agree that we each have our own values and definitions of success, one ingredient in the formula seems to be universal. It seems that people expect to achieve their best accomplishments independently without significant external support, as if seeking outside help would be cheating. They have difficulty owning their accomplishments if they received help along the way.

What I know is that success does not occur in a vacuum. Most people achieve success with assistance or other support systems that enable them to accomplish their goals.

I am not here to define what success is for you. In fact, I would expect that your goals and aspirations will change under different circumstances and over time. Therefore, it will serve you well if you keep your assumptions in check to allow your best thinking, performance, and energy to be applied without the shadow of expectations to cloud your process. You will be surprised what can occur when you stay open to the possibilities that may show up.

Ron Carucci

Ron Carucci has worked in more than twenty-five countries on four continents. He is the author of nine books, a two-time TEDx speaker, and is a regular contributor to the *Harvard Business Review* and *Forbes*. His ideas have been featured in *Fortune*, *CEO Magazine*, *Inc.*, *Business Insider*, MSNBC, and *Businessweek*. Ron is the co-founder and managing partner at Navalent, a consulting firm that provides customized organizational and leadership development solutions to their clients. Ron works with CEOs and executives pursuing transformational change for their organizations and industries. He has a thirty-year track record helping executives tackle challenges of strategy, organization, and leadership from start-ups to Fortune 10s, nonprofits to heads of state—including overseeing turnarounds, new markets, leadership overhauls, and culture changes to redesign for growth. Ron has helped clients articulate strategies that led to accelerated growth, enabling organizations to execute those strategies. He loves his work. So, how did he get there?

Ron's career began as a teenager in the performing arts. He went to college in New York City and pursued an acting career, but discovered quickly that he bored too easily even though he was getting great jobs. His friends were envious of his good fortune, yet he'd be thinking, *I have to do the same thing eight times a week for how long?* So, Ron left New York to go on tour with a repertory company that used media and the arts to do communications work, to see if that offered more variety. By working as both a performer and facilitator, he could test his theory that by seeing different parts of the world and using a variety of materials, he might find more engagement. Just twenty-four years old at this time, Ron got what he wished for when the company sent him to Germany under a contract with the US State Department.

 We were in Dachau, Germany, of all places, in this chapel. They didn't have terms like diversity and inclusion then. If they did, that's probably what this workshop would have been called. In the chapel were Germans and Americans. This was before the curtain fell. East and West Germany were on the horizon as one Germany. Civilians, military, State Department, and their spouses were in attendance to figure out how to create community together. In preparing for the workshop, we traveled to visit with the military guarding the border. There was a large field of barbed wire between East Germany and West Germany. I remember looking across, seeing an East German soldier and feeling this weird chill. It was my first time seeing someone from a Communist country. I asked a guard on our side what it was like to see them every day.

He said, 'It's not a big deal. At night we open the gates, and play soccer together.'

I said, 'Wait...what...aren't they the enemy?!'

He said, 'Nah, they're doing the same job just like we are.' It was an eye-opening moment.

Back in Dachau doing the workshop, a young soldier raised his hand and said, 'I'm just so tired of being trained to hate.' I felt alarmed and wondered, how does what we're doing here make him even think to say that? I wanted to know more. We had a great conversation with the group. I was so fascinated by his story and wanted to talk more about it. We went out for a beer and spoke for a few more hours. That was the moment I realized telling stories is interesting, but engaging people in their stories is fascinating work. I'll never be bored doing that. That was where my career shifted toward organizational psychology and leadership change work.

Ron returned to the US from Germany feeling more focused about his career. He was aware that there was a training and development field and an organizational development field, each with its own vocabulary and career path, and he was excited to go forward. He landed a position in the training and development department of a large energy company just outside New York City, where he remained for five years. Ron then moved on to earn his master's degree in organizational and human resource development, which enabled him to work as an internal consultant within several large corporations.

Over time, he experienced patterns as he did this type of work, noting, "Ancient wisdom says, you can't be a prophet in your own land."

Working inside an organization, Ron realized that just because people were asking for the truth, as in his honest feedback or insights, didn't mean they actually wanted to hear it. He admits that during those earlier years he may have been a little less diplomatic than he could have been. He reflected:

 I began to collect severance packages and realized that when I did this work inside companies, I got into trouble. When I did this outside of companies, I got paid really well, so maybe I should try that.

Ron gave it careful thought and decided to start his own consulting practice. About a year later, in his mid-thirties, Ron had what he calls a moment of brutal self-honesty. He realized that he could design effective leadership development programs and bring valuable organizational change initiatives to companies, but he knew he didn't have enough experience to work at the top of organizations, or to stay relevant for another thirty years. He said this was the most intentional moment he had experienced in his career. Ron believed consulting would have paid the bills, but it wasn't going to be really satisfying, given his level of expertise at that point. He worked with a mentor for a whole year and talked with some friends through a thoughtful process to identify what he was meant to be doing. Ron realized that he was at his best when he was working with senior executives who were facing extraordinary decisions. He was able to see the influence of his work, and the profound degree of transformation that resulted, yet he felt that he needed to be in an arena that

would enable him to grow his strengths further. Ron decided
to shut down his individual practice and accepted an invitation to join one of the most prestigious consulting firms in his
field. He says it was the best decision he ever made in his
career.

Ron gained the learning and depth that he had hoped to
at the new firm, and he remained there for eight years. Eventually, they were acquired by a much bigger firm. Ron and a
couple of colleagues felt that the work under the larger entity
was no longer fun. So they left and started their own firm,
Navalent, where Ron is one of the managing partners to this
day. Navalent works with leaders and their organizations to
develop strategies that enable them to implement transformational change.

 Isn't it funny how career stories are always
perfectly rational in retrospect? I can stitch
together the best narrative, but during that
period, it felt like the most unexpected, inelegant
rollercoaster of a career. There was nothing
coherent or elegant about most of the choices
that I made. I either volunteered to exit, or I was
'exited,' instead of saying this is the next right
move. I wished I had understood the importance
of crafting a career journey, but I didn't. Early in
our career, we obsess over the rest of our lives,
when we really should be thinking about our
opening moves. Then, we get into a rut and only
think about the next move, when we ought to be
thinking about the bigger story of our career.

As Ron reflects somewhat critically on the manner in
which he navigated his career journey, the steps he took
landed him in a place that many of us, including Ron himself,
would call successful and fortunate. His terms for success were

phrased as when "I am at my best," and he articulates what being at his best means to him:

- *When I am most joyful and feel pride and gratitude in my work*
- *When I feel like I'm making a difference*
- *When I have evidence that tells me my impact was sustained*

Ron has researched and written extensively about executive leadership development, organizational design and change, and strategy formulation. While he offers a great deal of data and analysis in his work, I am intrigued with the kinds of questions he asks and the way he makes me think. Ron takes nothing for granted and challenges conventional thinking—not in order to be a rebel, but to take an honest look at how we conduct ourselves and operate our organizations. His book, *Rising to Power*[1], is an excellent example of this. In it he writes about the importance of learning to adapt to change rather than applying a former successful strategy to the change. The past strategy cannot be implemented universally. He told me:

 You have to do your due diligence no matter what kind of transition you're looking to make. That points to some bad transitions I made in the past, because I didn't do any research first. I didn't really stop and think, what does that mean for me a year or two or even five years down the road? Not that I had a crystal ball, but how might I have formulated my choices differently from where I was, to what I think I would like my whole life to look like down the road, not just my job. I think I spent too much time making decisions to go away from something—but thought I was making decisions to go toward something.

Now I tell people, 'If you're thinking about a career change, give yourself twelve months to architect that change to do your research.' Really understand the implications of your choices and be thoughtful, because we all know you can go from the frying pan to the fire.

Ron admits that starting and running a firm for the past fifteen years happened by accident. Initially when he and his colleagues left their previous organization, they were planning to do contract work together, until they realized that to do the kinds of projects they wanted, they'd need more help. The projects kept coming in, and Navalent was born.

In addition to starting and growing Navalent, Ron also hired an executive coach, Dorie Clark, who he has worked with for more than five years. They have formed a strong working relationship, which Ron says has added tremendous, if not life-changing, value to his ability to move forward with a thoughtful approach to everything he does.

This points to an important lesson that most successful people acknowledge readily: They did not do it alone. As I always say, success does not occur in a vacuum.

Alisa Barcan

A few years ago, Alisa Barcan was living in Romania, pursuing her undergraduate studies in political science and international relations. She had absolutely no expectations that anything in her life would change, but it did so significantly.

Today, Alisa is a financial coach and consultant based in the UK. She works with professionals and small business owners who want to decipher their finances and improve their financial situation and relationship with money. She is a chartered certified accountant, a qualified coach from the University of Cambridge, UK, a contributor to *Harvard Business Review*, host of a YouTube channel, and teacher at the University of Cambridge, UK.

 If you would have asked me fifteen years ago if I would leave my country, that just wasn't an option, not because I didn't think I could do it, but I just never thought about it. So it happened that my fiancé got offered a PhD scholarship in the UK. And all of a sudden, I was like, I'm gonna have to move to this country. I moved to the UK just after finishing university, and until then, I had studied political science and international relations. It was 2007 when Romania entered the European Union, which was a very topical subject for us. And I thought, oh, yes, I'll be able to bring my contribution to Romania entering the EU, and I was really excited about it.

Once Alisa moved to the UK, she started a master's degree program in international political communication, advocacy, and campaigning. She completed her masters and found herself caught up in the bureaucracy of a new country joining the European Union. To qualify for employment in the UK, Alisa had to wait one year to secure a work permit. She found the waiting period to be challenging yet contemplative. During that time, Alisa did some volunteer jobs and worked with a career advisor, who had her take a full day of vocational tests.

When the test results came back, Alisa was surprised. There was nothing about politics. Most of the suggestions were finance related: bank underwriter, insurance broker, etc. The career advisor asked Alisa if she had ever considered working in finance.

No, she had never given a thought to a career in finance.

And the adviser said, "That's OK. You can join as a graduate, and they will teach you everything you need to know." Alisa initially was very confused by this and thought the advisor wasn't credible with this advice; this wasn't what she had chosen for herself. Then, she decided to reconsider the idea, thinking she would just apply to one job in finance. Alisa thought that if she were hired, it would be a sign that she ought to learn more about this type of work. If she didn't get the job, she would never give finance another thought.

Alisa applied for a finance role, which required taking competency tests. She passed with flying colors and received an offer.

The work permit arrived a few days after Alisa got the offer. It was such a stressful time. Alisa was the only candidate who applied for the role without a finance background, and she wasn't sure this would be the right career move for her.

 I said to myself, you know what? Now I've got the permit. If I don't like this job, I won't stay in it. I can always apply for other jobs. But I did like it. I liked it a lot. And immediately after I started, I was offered the opportunity to study for chartered accountancy and become a qualified accountant. So, I said yes to that. Two and a half years later, I was a qualified accountant.

At that juncture, Alisa needed to bring in income and would have taken any job. It just so happened that she landed a position within a company where she continued to grow for several years before eventually deciding not to practice accountancy anymore. Alisa realized it was important to identify what she enjoyed doing versus doing a job that she was just good at, because the practice of accountancy was no longer challenging enough. So after advancing through a few accountancy roles, Alisa was able to move into an assistant business analyst role in a department that was responsible for change management. While she still used her analysis and quantitative skills, it was a more dynamic position that involved interpersonal engagement and problem-solving.

Eight months later, Alisa found another job with a larger company and made the move into a business operations analyst role. The only finance person on the team, her job was to make sure that all the revenue they were generating was recorded and reported properly, and that nothing was missed. It was a big deal, to the extent that she became instrumental in preventing a seven-figure revenue loss in one year.

 I haven't had a huge corporate career, but I was lucky enough to not be completely unhappy in any of the roles that I've had. I'm very relentless in a way. When I get into a new job, it takes me about six months before I can do that job with no problem. And then I ask myself, now what? So, in my six-year career, I was doing an interview on average every six months. I just couldn't sit still long enough to see where the job would take me if there wasn't an apparent opportunity for me to take a step up. I think looking back, and we're all wiser in hindsight, I was looking for something in these jobs that I never was going to find unless I started my own business.

While Alisa has a quiet, non-confrontational manner, she owns that she is quite opinionated and feels strongly about the things that she wants to accomplish. She did not like having a boss. (I can relate to that!) Alisa much prefers the opportunity to implement an idea immediately and drive the work wherever she wants it to go. Of course, in a company, one can't just implement changes just because they think they're a good idea, even though they might create improved conditions. There's a budget and approval process that needs to happen before someone can do any of that. For Alisa, that process was just too long.

In 2018, Alisa enrolled in a year-long coaching qualification program at the University of Cambridge, after having launched her financial coaching business in 2017 while working full-time. She was consumed with everything she had taken on and it affected her social life, and everything else. Alisa even moved to a new job before she realized what the real issue was. The truth was that she needed to be 100 percent focused on her business rather than a company. It took time before the business was generating enough revenue for Alisa to be able to quit her job. She felt that it was important to take these steps wisely to set a good example as an accountant and financial coach. Alisa gave herself a two-year deadline to go into full-time self-employment, but she made it happen in just one year.

 So, 2017 was a very good year for me at work. Everyone was congratulating me and saying how proud they were of my results. All I could think of was: is this all there is? I struggled with that, because I had this good job. I was young, on an upward trajectory, and yet I was dissatisfied with my work, and there were no apparent reasons why I would be unhappy. So, I struggled with that for a while, and it took a lot of soul searching before I could find out what was bothering me. What bothered me the most was the impact that I was making was not significant enough, in my opinion. Although it was financially significant to the company, I didn't think that it was impacting anything else. When I discovered financial coaching, I thought this is it, this is what I want to do, yet I still wanted to be able to use the skills that I'd learned, just in a different capacity.

Along with providing financial coaching services, Alisa launched a YouTube channel in which she records a weekly video where she talks about money in a wider context. It's not just about personal and business finances, but she incorporates financial well-being topics. Since her goal is to impact as many people as she can, Alisa is excited to convey her messages on this platform.

Most recently, Alisa was invited to teach a class on small business finance at the University of Cambridge, where she earned her coaching credentials. The course is specifically for coaches, consultants, and service providers who are proficient at what they do but lack the business skills they need to build a financially viable business. Alisa brings together her skills and experiences as a coach and business owner to teach people how to create a healthy business from the start and not spend years struggling before they discover they could have done it more effectively.

Jay Vogt

Jay Vogt is the founder of Peoplesworth, an organizational development consulting practice serving mission-driven organizations, which he started in 1982. He has worked with nonprofits in healthcare, education, human services, arts, culture, environment, and fast-growth companies in the organic food world like Stonyfield and Applegate. Jay is a master facilitator of meetings and retreats, specializing in leading large groups of anywhere from 35 to 350 participants. A published author, Jay's TEDx talk on "The Art of Facilitation, Changing the Way the World Meets" has been viewed over 100,000 times.

I started my consulting practice when I was twenty-seven. The career path for that is usually one of two things. People either have a career in industry, and they then sell their experience, because they've been there and done that. Or they get an MBA, and they work for a consulting firm and fly all over the country. And they learn all these models, and then they go out on their own. I did neither of those things. I just jumped into private practice at a young age, which is very much against the odds and made my mother very nervous.

How did Jay arrive at opening a private practice so early in his career? To begin, Jay attended a unique undergraduate institution, Hampshire College—a small liberal arts college in Amherst, Massachusetts. Students earn their bachelor's degrees once they have completed a series of independent, interdisciplinary projects, a self-designed major, and a thesis. There are no grades, no tests, and no credits. Transcripts are a compilation of extensive written evaluations from faculty on the student's classwork or projects. (Full disclosure: I attended Hampshire a few years later.) To thrive at Hampshire, one must be highly self-motivated, independent, and ready to take on significant critical and analytical thinking in their academic endeavors. It's the kind of learning environment where asking skillful questions is valued more than needing to know everything ahead of time. The school's motto is *Non Satis Scire*, which is Latin for "to know is not enough." So that could partially explain why Jay was able to hang up his consultant's shingle at such an early stage in his career.

In his earliest years after graduation, Jay held a few unremarkable jobs, as he describes it. Then he went to work for a university extension service in Boston, where he focused on energy conservation in communities, introducing the use of solar power. He also became interested in how small nonprofits were training their boards of directors to function effectively. Jay developed training modules for new board members to be better oriented to their roles. He found this to be really interesting work.

These experiences enabled Jay to be in front of groups sharing information with the public while helping them to develop an understanding of their own needs. As a facilitator, he found that he could bring out the best in people and felt that his skills and talents came out naturally in these settings. Jay said he would literally feel himself vibrating in these situations and realized that he had a calling to do more of this work.

At that point, it felt clear that this is what he wanted to do with his life, yet he had no idea how to make money doing it, or what the career path looked like. Jay also felt that while his job allowed him to learn more about this kind of work, it remained quite peripheral to the core of what he really wanted to do. Yet he kept practicing and learning as best he could, even though he found the extension service to be very bureaucratic and not very customer focused or market driven. He knew it was not a place he could grow with over time.

 It was not only my first professional job, it was essentially my only job, because after that, I've been self-employed my entire life. It's an unusual way to go about doing this. I can't express how profound this shift was. I was really clear about what I wanted. But every time I imagined leaving my secure job to go out and start something, I imagined failure. I oscillated between wanting it and imagining it would work, wanting it and imagining it wouldn't work. It was working with a coach that helped me to stop the cycle. This person was paraphrasing my situation and said,

'What you want is to start your own practice, and you want it to be successful.' He said it's as if I didn't realize I could have both. Once I saw that I could have what I wanted, all of my energy lined up around this. I didn't have that oscillation anymore holding me back. So I picked a date, started my prep work, built my network, left the world of secure employment, and essentially never looked back.

In addition to his work with the coach, Jay shared that it was a profound act of trust to declare what he wanted, focus on it, and then to take actions in alignment with that goal—without any certainty that it would ultimately come to pass. With this, he points to the strength of his spiritual beliefs. Jay believes that there are some bigger forces at work, and that we're here on this planet for specific purposes. And when we are self-aware enough to calibrate where we invest our efforts—into things that are what we are meant to do—our energy lines up accordingly. So, the profound act of trust Jay points to comes from within himself and the "greater good" that drives his contributions. I would say that is an *inside out* way of working.

 The world is made up of jobs, and your identity is tied up in your work. That's one way of living life. It's self-identity with jobs. I left that and entered a river of projects with opportunities that emerge, and then they go away. Then, identity isn't defined by a particular job, because there's nothing that you're committed to 100 percent. In my case, I have all these different clients; they're coming and going. I noticed that every year, I had an anchor client, but each year it was different, it was the spookiest thing. A big project would emerge that would carry me through the year, and I would do other small things. The next year it would shift, and I couldn't control it. Yet I could kind of predict it, because there was this emergent quality of opportunities that I could gradually relax into trusting something would come out of it. That's not a great core for a business plan, but it is what my experience has been.

(Author note: My experience has been similar, having had an anchor client each year during my twenty plus years in business—it's uncanny! In my case, some of them were my clients for several years.)

In the early days of being self-employed, Jay made what he calls "smart choices." He bought a triple-decker (three-family home) in Boston which was in rough condition. He fixed it up and became a landlord, renting out two of the units while living in the third. Jay was doing a lot of "stand-up training," offering one- to three-day courses at companies for their employees. He was good at it, the demand was constant, but it was not his purpose or what he truly wanted to do.

While this work supplied half of his revenues at that time, Jay kept his eyes on the prize: a consulting practice of doing work that he was good at and loved. As he put it, he made a whole bunch of compromises and smart choices that related to the business side, while knowing that none of it guaranteed success. Over time, Jay says he learned to relax into the uncertainty—and started to enjoy that everything he did was not predictable or expected.

But even in the midst of this uncertainty, Jay created a brand and identity for his business that has remained solid and created threads of continuity throughout the years. He writes a regular newsletter and has built a deep network in his home city of Boston, Massachusetts, where he has focused on building a local practice.

It was so interesting to hear Jay talk about the compromises and "smart choices" he made that were so intrinsically linked to his goals. So often I listen to people talk about the compromises they are making in order to reach a long-range goal, usually a financial one, only to be living in a steady stream of pain that is clearly crushing their well-being and spirit in almost every other aspect of their lives. It's as if they could not envision a more satisfying path to reach that long-range goal.

 It did serve a purpose. It may not have been soulful, but to me, that's wisdom. I had a primary choice, which was to set up a practice that would feed my soul and serve my community. I was clear about that and I was making a secondary choice to do things I didn't want to do until I could realize my goal. The alternative was to not have money, to have a lot of fear, or to go backwards to a job. None of those things were better, and most seemed worse. If you are focused on what you want, and you know why you're making certain choices, you can find the fortitude to stick with it.

There was something else that Jay did intentionally from a place of passion with regard to his practice. He built his practice to be local and kept it that way, but not without some inner conflict. Jay was acutely aware of other consulting practices and how his colleagues were growing their businesses. Some of them went the route where they built a big office first and had a lot of overhead. Others went toward establishing a reputation nationally, and they could pick their clients, frequently traveling to get higher-status, higher-paying clients. While he saw male and female colleagues alike achieving these levels of growth, Jay shared that he felt wired to feel diminished by their success, as if by way of comparison he wasn't measuring up to their growth standards. While not proud of that feeling, he could own it for what it was, as so many men have been conditioned to go after the *bigger is better* route to success. Yet, Jay was making choices that felt right to him by staying local, as at this point, he was married and had a child. He wanted to be home for dinner at night, so he very persistently said yes to local work and turned down national work. Jay rejected the higher-status clients and the higher-paying fees, and opted out of going to national conferences, because that is where he would have met people from different places, and they would have wanted him to travel to conduct additional work for them.

 I built a practice that was focused locally. And it worked for me, but I also had to deal with this voice in my head saying I wasn't being successful. So I redefined success. I went on a search for a model that would tell me I was doing the right thing. And being a New Englander, I came upon the image of the country doctor who is a professional, works in one area with the same people over many years, and gets to know them extremely well. They are trusted and even revered in their community, but never go outside of that community. I said, well, that's it. I'm a country doctor for the clients that I serve in Boston. And just that wiring of my brain—my male brain allowed me to calm down and just enjoy the fact that I had a home office, was home for dinner, and could see my daughter. I was never getting on planes. That really worked for me. And fast forward years later, I saw many of those same consultants I admired. They got divorced, or they burnt out. And some of them took me aside and said, 'We really envy what you have, and wish we would have made different choices.' Isn't that interesting? I was blown away by that.

It took years for Jay to truly tackle his own demons about what success meant to him, and once he felt more grounded, other discoveries started to emerge. He found that there's a freedom to design a life that is unrestrained of other strictures. He and his family started doing things that people don't do all the time. His wife was a teacher in a private school, so Jay started mimicking her time off and took time away from his business during those periods, so that they could travel and spend time together as a family. Later, they did something they always wanted to do. Jay and his wife saved money for two years and took a five-month sabbatical to travel all around Asia.

Once the news was out about their plans, a trusted colleague of Jay's pulled him aside one day, looked him in the eye, and said, "You're committing economic suicide, the idea of walking away from a practice for five or six months."

Jay responded with his motto, "I may not ever retire, but I'm going to retire a little bit all the way along."

Surprisingly enough, Jay's clients embraced his plans with admiration, and all returned to him once he was back in town. And that was just the first of several sabbaticals Jay has taken over the years while serving as a "country doctor."

 My practice became like slowly pruning a plant. I would leave, come back, and things would get stronger—which was counterintuitive. But that kind of feedback—that if you do something that feels really right, even if it's unconventional— something good can come out of it. It started making me think, what else could I design in my life? I'm making choices around the location, around time, around family, around the mission, and the work that I'm doing. It isn't just self-serving. I need to be present to serve my clients, because they're overwhelmed, exhausted, and they have a million things going on. If I'm like that, I can't give any service to them. So I tell people, 'I'm doing this for you.' So there's a business rationale of self-investment that pays dividends. We are governed by a whole set of rules about how we are supposed to live that we don't even know are shaping us. When someone in the tribe goes off and does something a little different, people say, 'Wow, is that even possible? It looks like something I might like to do, but I've never given myself permission.'

In his fifties, Jay started looking ahead to a time in life when he would want to do less consulting and have other things occupy his time. He started an internet-based business called EssentialWorth, a virtual consultancy that helps nonprofits experience affordable board and strategic planning. Another business he has is a real estate development company in Mexico with a couple of partners. Jay says, "Even late in life, we can make big and bold choices, try different things, take some risks, learn new skills and some new tricks, even as an old dog."

One of Jay's inspirations is the poet David Whyte; and in the vein of our podcast conversation, he shared this excerpt from one of Whyte's poems, which captures the essence of how Jay has made choices in his career and life.

You must learn one thing:
the world was made to be free in.
Give up all the other worlds
except the one to which you belong.

Sometimes it takes darkness and the sweet
confinement of your aloneness
to learn

anything or anyone
that does not bring you alive
is too small for you.

— EXCERPTED "SWEET
DARKNESS" FROM *THE HOUSE OF
BELONGING* BY DAVID WHYTE

Ron, Alisa, and Jay each traveled their own distinct paths to find meaning and satisfaction in their careers. While they grew as people and as professionals, their lives and needs changed. This was reflected in the ways they made decisions and the subsequent steps they took. Each of them navigated through various trials and tribulations as tested by their values, maturity, preferences, and strengths.

Their stories tell us different scenarios of success, don't they? For each of them, there was an ebb and flow of achieving success until they felt compelled or had to make their next move. Too often, I believe, we discuss success as if it were a finite accomplishment or endpoint to be realized. Then if we have not reached a certain pinnacle, however we define it, we cannot declare ourselves "successful." Perhaps this is an exaggeration, but I do think this idea drives the mindsets of many ambitious professionals who want to do something that matters. I hear it in the questions, expectations, and disappointments that my clients express regularly with regard to where they see themselves today—versus where they thought they would be or believe they ought to be at this juncture in their career.

So, what is it that we are aiming for in our work, career, or livelihood? Is it to *be* a success, as a thing? To arrive *at* success, as a place? To have *achieved* success as a measurement, benchmark, or endpoint? While there may not be one answer here, it does seem that we are trying to reach for something we can feel good if not great about in our careers.

We need to accept that we won't always make the right decisions,
that we'll screw up royally sometimes – understanding that
failure is not the opposite of success, it's part of success.

—Arianna Huffington

Reflective Questions and Guiding Activities

In answering the following questions, reflect on the moments, situations or experiences that you would identify as having been successful in your life. Would you still see them that way today? Have your criteria for success changed over time? Going forward, how you would like to feel about your professional or personal contributions?

Self-Assessment

On a scale of 1 (not satisfied) to 10 (completely satisfied), how satisfied are you in your career or current work role?

What does your score mean to you? Be as specific as possible in articulating your feelings and thoughts the areas of satisfaction or dissatisfaction in your career or current role.

Assuming your score is two to three points higher, what would your career or current role look like in terms of your thoughts, feelings, and activities?

What kinds of information, relationships, or opportunities do you imagine are available to you at this higher score?

What might get in the way or prevent you from elevating your score? Name as many concerns or obstacles as you can.

What actions can you take to raise your score in the next six months to one year? It may help to speak about your options with a trusted colleague, or friend to percolate a few ideas, or hire a coach to explore your options in more depth.

Here are some suggested activities that you can try to move your professional journey forward:

Write Your Eulogy

This is an exercise that has been used in both personal growth and professional development programs. It is important to follow these instructions as closely as possible so that you can get what you need from this activity. Plan ahead to spend a few uninterrupted hours on this, preferably in a new spot that will offer you fresh surroundings but no distractions. There are two parts to this exercise.

1. Write as if your eulogy is being delivered today. Your life ended two days ago. Imagine the room full of people at your memorial service. Who is there? Where are they seated and with whom? Be completely honest with yourself. What would be the opening sentence in your eulogy? What would those closest to you say about how you lived, your values, your character, what you gave to them and what they will miss about you? Take a good look throughout the rows of seats. Is there anyone missing? Of the people who are there, who are they there for? Are there any surprises as you look across the room? How would you close the eulogy?

2. Write your eulogy as you hope it would be in the future when you actually pass away. How would you like to be

remembered? What is the legacy you want to leave behind after you go? Refer to the questions in part 1 to create this eulogy.

Join or Create a Peer Mastermind Group

A mastermind group is a group of peers who meet regularly to give each other guidance and support around goals and challenges. People find professionally themed mastermind groups to be a great source of support, resources, motivation, and accountability in attaining their career growth goals. Groups are often formed by the members themselves. Starting with a theme, they create a set of guidelines by which the group operates, ensuring accountability and a foundation for making productive use of their time together. Some groups are facilitated by a professional who offers additional content and potentially coaching on a group or individual basis as part of a packaged program. Information about how to form and run an effective mastermind group is readily available on the internet.

YOU NEED TO NETWORK, BUT NOT JUST FOR A JOB

Networking remains the number one cause of job attainment.

—HAL LANCASTER

According to Merriam-Webster, the definition of *networking* is "the exchange of information or services among individuals, groups, or institutions; specifically: the cultivation of productive relationships for employment or business."[1]

Networking gets a bad rap. It is often misconstrued as an uncomfortable or awkward social activity that requires making small talk, or engaging in the disingenuous exchange of business cards. Yet effective networking encompasses a variety of activities with far-reaching benefits. For anyone who wants to make a career or job change, it is vitally important to understand how networking, in its many forms, is the most powerful strategy for creating positive results.

It's not what you know but who you know. That's a phrase that reminds us that life isn't always fair. Yet, there is something positive in that statement that has been true for a long time. It does matter who you know. We refer to them as word-of-mouth or warm connections. There is no better way to get on-the-ground information about industries, a company's culture, or the hidden job market than from someone connected to the source of your interest. Marketing research has proven this over and over again. People make purchasing decisions based on friends' experiences or ratings posted by customers. Guess what?! Those reviews and recommendations are a version of networking. Referrals, recommendations, or "putting in a good word" for somebody are solid everyday networking examples. Yet, in the context of a job search or asking people for help, you can employ many strategies to build your network and gain the information you need to move forward with your plans.

There are three buckets I suggest you examine with regard to your relationship with networking: *mindset, feelings,* and *approaches.* Think about how each of these can help or hinder the chances of achieving your goals, whether short or long-term, modest or lofty, career-focused or personally driven.

Mindset

There's an inner narrative, a driver, that I refer to as our mindset, a set of ideas, expectations, or assumptions about something that shapes our thoughts, feelings, and behaviors about it. Our mindset applies to how we approach network-ing, often in a way that limits our ability to make the most of our connections. It is essential to be aware of our assump-tions about networking to move our careers in a meaningful direction. One way to keep your mind fresh and ready for opportunities is to stay open and curious about the people and world around you. Retain a glass-half-full kind of aware-ness; keep asking questions to ensure you have the information you need to have the options and choices you would like.

Feelings

I have already noted some of the typical negative feelings that occur when people think about networking. Making the most of your networking efforts helps to be aware of how you feel about yourself in relation to the activities and people you will engage. Are you nervous, excited, frightened, overwhelmed, or delighted about meeting new people, reconnecting with former colleagues, learning about recent developments in your field, or sharing that information with others? A wide range of emotions may strike you when encountering new people, former connections, cutting-edge information, and fresh approaches to challenging problems. In one form or another, networking is often the avenue to making progress—by engaging in relationships and acquiring new information that can inform their choices and next moves.

Approaches

Networking, in my opinion, boils down to two essential key functions: relationship building and research. By engaging in exchanges of information with trusted colleagues and other people, you are gaining key knowledge that will inform your career pursuits. Many of my clients initially viewed networking as a finite activity to learn about a job posting or as a special request for help. Still, there are tremendous benefits offering value that can last a lifetime.

The primary approach to networking is developing connections with other people—and building relationships that can offer the information, additional contacts, or resources to support your professional goals. We have a multitude of ways to make these connections through networking events and groups, social media applications such as LinkedIn, introductions through existing relationships, and serendipitous situations in which we happen to "be at the right place, at the right time." Your network of contacts can include former co-workers, classmates, friends, acquaintances, and family. The only limitations to the list are the ones you place on it. Remember my client Keith in Chapter Two? When I sense a client's discomfort in reaching out for help, I suggest the 'if the table were turned' scenario to them, and they readily admit they would be happy to assist anyone who asks for help.

The succession of starting with a closer connection and being introduced to additional people from that point expands your network—which eventually leads to gaining information that helps accomplish your goals. Research has shown that 80–85 percent[2] of people find their next job through this kind of networking; surprisingly, it can be through a fourth- or fifth-degree contact that an actual position is secured. Networking and creating connections can feel like a numbers game, but if executed with consistency *and* patience, the results are meaningful and satisfying.

The two people I profile in this chapter offer excellent examples of how networking can help you move your life in fulfilling directions. Robbie Samuels, who has been named a networking expert, describes himself as an "extroverted extro-vert." Dorie Clark, an introvert, is a highly skilled and successful networker. Both of them deeply value a variety of networking activities for building rewarding and productive relationships that are integral to their lives and businesses.

Robbie Samuels

Robbie Samuels's connection to networking and forming strategic relationships goes back to his roots and has evolved over time as he found his way to becoming a keynote speaker, virtual event design consultant, and relationship-based business strategist.

 I fell in love with event planning at a young age and organized friends my whole life. It took me a while to realize that it was a career. In high school, for a senior trip, I asked, 'How many seats are on a bus?' Fifty-six. I got fifty-six of my friends on the same bus. If there was an opportunity to organize and make a better experience for my friends, I did it.

Robbie's love of community organizing led him to get his master's degree in social work, focusing his studies on groups and communities. In his second year, he secured an internship opportunity to serve as the New York State coordinator for a national LGBTQ visibility campaign.

That internship led Robbie on a fifteen-year path working for LGBTQ and HIV/AIDS nonprofits. In 2002, he moved to Boston and volunteered at an AIDS Walk, where he met the event staff. They remembered him a couple of months later when he applied and was hired to be the logistics manager of their organization's charity bike ride. When that contract position ended, two colleagues recommended him to work with a national LGBTQ conference that he had attended several times since his college days. Robbie had always gone out of his way to engage with the conference director and years later when he was recommended to her, she remembered him—despite the fact that he is transgender and had changed quite a bit since she had last seen him.

When the conference position ended, Robbie received a panicked call from an LGBTQ arts organization in need of last-minute support for their annual fundraising event. It was an organization that he had volunteered for in the past, which is why they thought of him. They even offered him a job at the end of the short contract, but he knew he wanted to be part of a bigger development team. When asked if he wanted a full-time role at the organization, Robbie said, "You really can't afford me. I'll probably only be able to remain here for a year if you're paying me, but I'll volunteer for ten years if you don't."

So that's what he did, he turned down this sure thing, because he wanted to be a special events manager for a larger, mission-driven organization. Robbie got his wish when a job he applied to six months earlier had been reposted. It was his dream job: special events manager at Gay & Lesbian Advocates & Defenders (GLAD). He applied again, and this time a different manager was screening applications. It turned out that the manager's wife had met Robbie at a networking event and had a positive impression of him. That apparently helped to move his resume to the top of the pile.

While he had been comfortable jumping from one contract job to another during those years, Robbie was now committed to working for one organization and thought he would be at GLAD for the rest of his life. This was his mindset when he took the role, in contrast to the typical two- to three-year tenure for special event managers. Robbie remained there for ten years, organizing approximately twenty-five events each year that raised about a million dollars. Eventually he was promoted to the senior manager of events and donor engagement.

A year after starting at GLAD, Robbie founded a Meetup group called Socializing for Justice (SoJust). SoJust was a cross-cultural, cross-issue progressive community and network in Boston. Over the next eleven years, Robbie grew the group to over 3,000 members and hosted hundreds of events before closing the group in 2017. The relationships he built through this group would later be the network he counted on when he took a leap of faith and left the security of a full-time job to become an entrepreneur. That part of his journey started with pro bono talks about networking—which became an official side hustle in 2009, when he started getting paid to speak to nonprofit boards and foundation grantees.

Early in 2015, Robbie became a full-time entrepreneur. He was now married and thinking about a future family, knowing he would never be home if he kept up the pace of fifty-plus events a year.

I first met Robbie in late 2016. His name was familiar to me, as it had regularly shown up in my inbox where posts about SoJust events were on various email lists. We connected through the global Recognized Expert community, which is composed of people enrolled in Dorie Clark's "How to Become a Recognized Expert" course. Robbie invited me to a monthly networking dinner he hosted in Boston—and a rich, rewarding, collegial relationship and friendship began. Robbie was an inspirational and tactical influence on my 2018 podcast launch. He is the host of *On the Schmooze*, a weekly podcast that features talented professionals sharing untold stories about leadership and networking. (I was honored to be his guest, episode 122.)

In 2016, Robbie was writing his first book, *Croissants vs. Bagels: Strategic, Effective and Inclusive Networking at Conferences*[3], and building his business. It wasn't overnight, but in the ten years since his first paid speaking gig, he did gain recognition as a networking expert—with numerous mentions in publications such as *Inc., Harvard Business Review, Forbes,* and *Fast Company.* He was also featured in two books, *Stand Out, How to Find Your Breakthrough Idea and Build a Following Around It*[4] by Dorie Clark, and *The Connectors Advantage: 7 Mindsets to Grow Your Influence and Impact*[5] by Michelle Tillis Lederman. All of his hard work was paying off, and he was even given an opportunity in 2019 to deliver an engaging TEDx talk titled, "Hate Networking? Stop Bageling and Be the Croissant!"

Then in March 2020, it became clear to Robbie that the

world was changing in dramatic ways due to the COVID-19 pandemic. Events were being canceled or postponed; a few were hastily brought online. For over a decade, Robbie had been working to establish his credibility as a networking expert with a focus on in-person networking. Suddenly, his expertise was no longer relevant. He was struggling with how he could "show up" and add value in a world that no longer valued the skill set he had so carefully developed.

> Who needed to know about body language and handshakes when we were not supposed to be gathering in groups anymore?

Robbie jumped into action and wrote an article, "9 Ways to Network in a Pandemic." He posted it across social media and to his blog and then decided to follow his own advice. By Friday, March 13, 2020, he hosted his first Virtual Happy Hour; this morphed quickly into his free weekly #NoMore-BadZoom Virtual Happy Hour, which he has hosted weekly since then.

Quickly and instinctively, Robbie reinvented his business without having a clear sense of what was next. His entrepreneurial spirit helped him recognize new opportunities, and his extensive network was at his fingertips—ready to receive what he had to offer. Everyone at this point was staying close to home, on their computers, and craving connection. He became a virtual event design consultant and executive Zoom producer helping national and statewide advocacy organizations bring their events online. In May 2020, he created a virtual event professional #NoMoreBad-Zoom certification program to train speakers and event professionals on how to use digital and analog tools to design and execute engaging online experiences.

What Robbie didn't realize in mid-March as his business came to an abrupt halt was that he had adjacent expertise that was highly valuable in this newer digital world. He was very comfortable online and had years of practice with online facilitation of masterminds, group coaching, and training. Robbie also had experience teaching about productivity tech tools, which he enjoyed.

According to Robbie, the key to successful networking is being inclusive and welcoming. His experience hosting a podcast and interviewing hundreds of guests meant he could quickly build rapport and ask thoughtful follow-up questions. With every networking situation, you have the opportunity to play "host" and draw people together, building lasting relationships for yourself and others. You do not actually need to be hosting the event to step into this role. Being a host means creating a space that welcomes others; by taking on that role, you bring people together. For example, when going to a conference, Robbie will invite a group of people to join him for dinner at a local restaurant and facilitate a conversation at dinner which is both engaging and feels host-like. He also teaches people to create physical space, a "croissant" (a circle with an opening) within small groups at larger events, so that people feel comfortable joining a conversation.

To make great connections at meetings, events, and conferences requires having a strong sense of purpose going in and a system for staying connected afterward. Robbie's advice and guidance empowers people to have the mindset, approach, and tools to make relationship-building a reality.

With his love of events, experience with community-building, and a deep belief that events are about content *and* connection—it seems inevitable that Robbie would now be leading a virtual happy hour that has attracted an international group of over 1,200 registrants and fifty to sixty attendees each week. That community has been the referral engine that helped him quickly scale his business in just nine months from a cold start in April 2020.

But was it a cold start? Not at all...all of the people

Robbie has met over the last two decades are part of the vast network of connections he nurtures and sustains. He would be the first person to tell you that his network was the igniter for his quick reinvention.

Dorie Clark

Dorie Clark is what she calls "an overnight success ten years in the making." Dorie helps individuals and companies get their best ideas heard in a crowded, noisy world. She has been named one of the top fifty business thinkers in the world by Thinkers50, a UK-based business that focuses on "identifying, ranking, and sharing the leading management ideas of our age." Dorie was honored as the number one communication coach in the world by the Marshall Goldsmith Leading Global Coaches Awards, and one of the top 50 communication professionals in the world by Global Gurus, a research organization that utilizes specific criteria to select people who achieve superior results in their work, while developing and influencing professionals and organizations throughout the globe.

Today, Dorie is a keynote speaker and teaches executive education for Duke University's Fuqua School of Business and Columbia Business School. She is the author of *The Long Game, Entrepreneurial You, Reinventing You,* and *Stand Out,* which was named the number one leadership book of the year by *Inc.* magazine. Dorie has been described by the *New York Times* as an expert at self-reinvention and helping others to make changes in their lives. I can attest to that, because I am one of those people she has helped. She is also a frequent contributor to the *Harvard Business Review, Newsweek,* and *Fast Company.*

You may wonder how Dorie got to the top of all those lists. She is naturally brilliant and talented in many ways, and she has applied herself in a focused and thoughtful manner to everything she does while taking nothing for granted. While

Dorie is a self-described introvert, she has intentionally developed thousands of professional relationships that have resulted in a wide variety of beneficial connections over the years.

 As a kid, I was always writing stories, and I went to a writer's camp. My parents would go to a beach house. I thought it was the most boring thing in the world. I did not want to go to the beach. So the only way that I could get through these incredibly boring stints was I would demand that my mother buy me a big thick book called the Writer's Market, that would tell you where to submit your writing. As an eleven-year-old, you are not qualified to submit to them, but I was captivated with the idea of getting published. I would pour over it and write all kinds of stories, because I dreamed of being able to submit things. I was the twelve-year-old that was sending poems to the New Yorker. Shockingly, they were not interested in any of them.

Academically, Dorie was gifted. She completed her undergraduate studies in philosophy at eighteen and immediately continued with her graduate studies at Harvard Divinity School, earning her master's degree in theology at twenty-one. Dorie chose theology, as she viewed it as a "close cousin" to philosophy; she also was very interested in politics and advocacy. She was intrigued by how religion was playing out in American public life, so she focused her master's degree primarily on the history and sociology of American religion.

 I learned a lot about how the pieces fit together and wanted to be able to trace back the culture more. I had been passionate about politics and done political advocacy in college and grad school. In college, I managed to talk my way onto the board of directors of the Gay and Lesbian Victory Fund, now known as the Victory Fund, which is a political action committee for openly LGBTQ candidates. I had no business being on the board, because I had no money to give; so to justify my presence, I volunteered on the campaigns of candidates they endorsed. There were many people in Boston where I was living that they had endorsed. I got a lot of campaign experience and met many people. As a result, my resume included campaign work, which helped me get a job as a political reporter, because I understood the beat and had contacts there. Those relationships and emerging connections were critical to how I could advance myself as I developed new opportunities going forward.

Dorie's first job out of graduate school was working in Boston as a political reporter for a weekly newspaper. It was a good starting place for her career, as it laid the foundation for many other things that would follow. Unfortunately, there were some budget cuts at the paper, and Dorie was laid off on September 10, 2001. That's right, it happened the day before September 11, 2001. In the face of her own sudden circumstance—layered with the uncertainty of a national crisis—Dorie was alarmed, to say the least, at the prospect of finding another job.

The world was standing still. Nobody was hiring. Dorie had to scramble as the paper had laid her off with just four days' pay. One of her editors was able to introduce her to an editor at *The Boston Globe*, who hired her for some freelance assignments. Dorie also reached out to her network of connections from her prior campaign work and this helped her maintain a fairly steady flow of freelance writing projects for the next six months. While it did not feel good to her at the time, Dorie reflects on this period as a good training ground for entrepreneurship.

> It kind of kicked off my first reinvention journey. Being a freelance writer is exactly like being an entrepreneur. You have to understand with absolute certainty what your customer, meaning the editor, will be interested in. You must pitch it to them, sell it, and deliver it quickly. You do that over and over again, until you develop an instinctive sense of what the customer wants. If you don't get what they want, you're not going to make your rent money. I became a high stakes version of myself, learning to pivot and adapt— all the skills that an entrepreneur needs to have.

In an unexpected turn of events, Dorie ended up joining a political campaign. Her intention had been to continue freelancing until *The Boston Globe* could hire her full-time, as they were indicating their interest, but they had a hiring freeze. Dorie really wanted to grow her career as a journalist.

She got a call from someone in her network who had just become a consultant to Robert Reich, the former US labor secretary who was running for governor of Massachusetts. He asked Dorie if she was interested in being considered for a press secretary job. At first she said no because she was really intent on remaining a journalist; but then Dorie realized that working for Robert Reich was a big opportunity that she probably should not turn down in favor of waiting for something that may not happen. She called her contact back, they hired her, and she started the job. It had been six months since her layoff from the newspaper.

There were five candidates running, so it was a highly competitive race; and unfortunately, Reich lost in the primary.

Six months later and with no regrets, Dorie returned to free-lancing.

Through all of her campaign experiences, Dorie was able to expand her network significantly. The opportunity was ripe for meeting leaders and influential people from a cross section of representative groups that wanted to support the candidate and get their interests noticed. In the process, Dorie had built a large network and was skilled in managing those relation-ships in positive, productive ways.

In addition to freelancing, Dorie started consulting a few days a week at a PR firm in Boston, while she began to plan her next moves. She determined that she would like to work on a presidential campaign.

 I was trying very hard to get in. You have to work a million angles. There's not a very clear path to getting on a presidential campaign. You have to network like a fiend, which meant talking to lots of people and asking those people to steer me towards the right people and in the right direc-tions, and on and on. Eventually I was able to get hired on the Howard Dean campaign, which is where I spent most of 2003 and part of 2004. It was a tremendous learning experience and incredibly intense. Of course, it was not what I hoped in the sense that I hoped we would win.

Dorie said the campaign was hard living. She worked seven days a week, thirteen hours a day, under high stress. There was a sense that everything was of great historic impor-tance, so that when she started to feel run down, it took her two months before she went to a doctor to get badly needed antibiotics.

After fulfilling her goal to work on a presidential campaign, Dorie found herself feeling drawn to many causes.

Her career as a journalist was no longer front and center. She decided that she wanted to either run a small nonprofit or be the head of communications for a large nonprofit. If you haven't gathered this by now, not only is Dorie intellectually gifted, but she also possesses a fortitude and confidence that enables her to be proactive and think big. She also had developed an extensive personal and professional network in which she was as generous in helping others as she was resourceful in asking people for information and referrals.

Through a referral, Dorie was interviewed and hired as the executive director of a small nonprofit called the Massachusetts Bicycle Coalition—a statewide, bicycle lobbying organization. She worked with the state highway department to get roadways designed to be more bicycle-friendly, on policy changes to allow bikes on the subway system in Boston, and with the Department of Conservation and Recreation around the creation of bike paths around the state. Dorie discovered that while the hours were better in this role, her stress level was higher, because she was responsible for the fate of this organization and its employees.

 But I was very proud. I had to learn a lot of things, really be a jack of all trades. So it prepared me for entrepreneurship. I felt very good that I left it on a stable footing. The last big thing that I insisted we do before I left was embark upon a very aggressive direct mail campaign, which we had never done before. We were able to double the size of the membership base, so we were able to create something long-lasting to be passed on to my successor.

Dorie never thought about working for herself. Yet, about a year into working for the Massachusetts Bicycle Coalition, she had a sudden and powerful realization that running a little nonprofit—having to do all the different things and learn about every moving part—is just like running a business. And then she told herself, *I could run my own business.* So, she spent her second year at Mass Bike—planning, plotting it out, and educating herself about what it would take to start a business and eventually transition into it.

Originally, Dorie's vision was to start a business offering political consulting, because it was most closely related to what she had been doing recently. And she knew some political consultants, whom she viewed as solid role models who were making a good living. Dorie was confident in her ability to reach her goals, but once she launched and told people that she was on her own, she didn't get any political clients right away. She had a lot of small businesses and nonprofits that wanted to hire her as a communications consultant, so Dorie embraced that work.

Since her initial business launch in 2006, Dorie has written four books. Her first one was *Reinventing You: Define Your Brand, Imagine Your Future*[6], "a step-by-step guide to help you assess your unique strengths, develop a compelling personal brand, and ensure that others recognize the powerful contribution you can make." Writing and getting published was part of Dorie's reinvention strategy to expand the reach and scope of her business, as she saw the changing landscape of communications and how she could most effectively serve her clients. She also was conscious of the dynamic of being a hands-on consultant earning transactional revenue (meaning you work, you get paid; you don't work, you don't get paid), leaving her vulnerable to the shifting trends in the marketplace and economy. Dorie was fully committed to remaining self-employed and made the conscious choice to move from Boston to New York City to broaden her network.

Her next book, *Stand Out: How to Find Your Breakthrough Idea and Build a Following Around It*[7], grew out of the lessons learned and practices she implemented as she decided to scale and shape her business going forward. Dorie wanted to work with clients nationally and internationally while diversifying her revenue streams. New York was a better base from which to build this foundation. She continues to work under the umbrella of Clark Strategic Communications, and as the world changes continually, she keenly observes it to identify needs as they arise, so that she can address them strategically.

Dorie's third book, *Entrepreneurial You: Monetize Your Expertise, Create Multiple Income Streams, and Thrive*[8], further outlines the key principles and proven practices that she has implemented successfully to grow her business. She has built a huge body of work, now known under her brand as "Dorie Clark," including thousands of published articles in *Harvard Business Review, Fortune, Fast Company, Newsweek, Entrepreneur,* and *Inc.* She also offers online courses, does TEDx talks, teaches at several prominent business schools such as Duke and Columbia, and is booked for speaking internationally. Dorie also offers premium, highly targeted, individual coaching and small mastermind groups for entrepreneurs and executives.

As of writing this book, I have been a member of Dorie's Recognized Expert community for five years. (We call ourselves RExers.) It is the most interesting, smart, engaging, and generous group of professionals I have ever been involved with in my twenty plus years as an entrepreneur. We come from all over the world and represent a wide array of disciplines and areas of expertise. I always love to hear stories of "How did you meet or find Dorie?"

This is the essence of networking, dear readers: the stories of how people find each other, make connections, help each other out, share resources and experiences, and make introductions. The ways in which my network has expanded across the globe in the past five years and how that has impacted my business are tremendous.

If someone is thinking about trying to map out their next step, I would say to keep in mind that we often think about reinvention as a one-time thing—a big break in our lives. There is a way that we can actually be making small changes so that it's not such a huge titanic kind of experience, but instead we just keep pushing ourselves in small ways, so that we are ready to put our vision into action when we need to.

In her fourth book, *The Long Game: How to Be a Long-Term Thinker in a Short-Term World* [9], Dorie offers unique principles and frameworks that readers can apply incrementally to experience long-term gains in their personal and professional lives.

Dorie also offers a free reinvention self-assessment which is a helpful tool for anyone wanting to identify the areas they need to address as they go forward. You can find it here: https://dorieclark.com/reinvent along with many other great resources.

Both Robbie and Dorie effectively exercised the power of networking to grow their careers and expand their interests. While they each have their own distinct style of approaching the process, they have engaged in similar activities. When Dorie was still living in Boston, she and Robbie were friends and co-hosted dinners together to grow their networks. Now, each in different cities, they invite a small group of curated people to a restaurant for a casually facilitated dinner conversation. I have attended some of these dinners, meeting people I would never have gotten to know otherwise. Some have become guests on my podcast, others have hired me as their coach and many have remained colleagues, and friends in my network.

It's time we stretch our individual definitions of what it means to network as an action and to have a network as a web of people we feel connected to across various parts of our lives. Networking, in all of its forms, is *the* most important activity you will engage in to make meaningful connections and changes that can support your professional growth. In the Resources section of this book you will find a list of my favorite books on the practice of networking. Like exercising muscles, the more you connect with people in your networks, the better your outcomes will be—and the further you will see the vast benefits gained as a result.

Stay open and curious! Your mindset is the key to open the door to your next move.

Everyone you will ever meet knows something you don't.

—Bill Nye

Reflective Questions and Guiding Activities

Networking is the practice of engaging in productive relationships to gather information, enabling you to assess your options and make educated choices about your career or any other important matters in your life. You might access your network to get recommendations for physicians, contractors or lawyers, for example. The key is to learn new information or see things you already were familiar with in a new way so that you can determine if they are aligned with your interests, needs and values. It is also an opportunity to enjoy relationships with colleagues who you can be helpful to as well. Networking is at its finest when it operates like a two-way street throughout your career journey.

Self-Assessment

On a scale of 1 (extremely uncomfortable) to 10 (completely comfortable), what is your general comfort level with engaging your network to support your career goals?

What does your score mean to you? Be as specific as possible in articulating your feelings and thoughts about your experiences in particular networking situations or activities.

If your chosen score was two to three points higher than your original score, what would your experience look like in terms of your thoughts, feelings, and activities related to networking?

What kinds of information, relationships, or opportunities do you imagine are available to you at this higher score?

What might get in the way or prevent you from elevating your score?

What actions can you take to raise your score in the next three to six months? If you have difficulty thinking about your options, speak with a trusted colleague or friend to percolate a few ideas.

Here are a few proven approaches that have been effective for a multitude of professionals:

Host a dinner

This is a low cost (attendees pay their own check) option. Many people prefer small groups to large events. If you invited six to eight people to dinner to share ideas, resources, and conversation, who would be at the table? What would you like to learn from them?

Ask for an introduction

Ask friends, extended family, and colleagues (past and present), based on their knowledge of your background, interests, and goals, if they know people who would be good for you to speak with. Clarify that you are seeking information, not asking for a job reference. If there is a job posting or company you are targeting, you should disclose your specific interest and share your questions upfront.

Participate in professional groups or communities

LinkedIn, Facebook, Meetup.com, associations, or community-based groups—they may be industry-focused or role-specific associations that have local chapters. Join multiple groups on LinkedIn, and be active in those groups where you can share and gain the information or contacts that are of greatest interest to you. "Like" other members' posts, *and* offer comments on them. When posting your own content, be sure to also post a comment below, and tag people or organizations that may be interested. They will be notified that you acknowledged them in the post. This level of activity will boost your visibility on LinkedIn.

While larger groups and meetings can be very productive in making the connections needed to learn new information and develop strategic relationships, you should not feel as if you *have to* attend them. If you do go, however, have a plan for how you will engage people, so that when you leave, you will feel as if you made a good choice to attend the event. A great resource for large event networking is Robbie Samuel's book, *Croissants vs. Bagels: Strategic, Effective, and Inclusive Networking at Conferences.*

Create a Tracking System

I encourage all of my clients to create a tracking system to manage their network engagement, particularly during a job search. Spreadsheets or the use of a relational database such as a CRM (customer relationship management) system to keep track of people, contact information, links, important dates, and additional data helps them to stay focused and organized. By having all this information in one place, you will be able to efficiently attend to the "care and feeding" of your network, including sending thank-you and follow-up notes or referrals. These are a crucial part of the give-and-receive nature of effective networking.

I'M NOT QUALIFIED. DO I BELONG HERE?

*The willingness to consider possibility requires
a tolerance of uncertainty.*

—RACHEL NAOMI REMEN

Have you ever read an intriguing job description that caught your attention and thought: *They will never consider me. I don't have the qualifications or experience they are seeking.* Probably multiple times...

You pass on applying for the job, feeling a little deflated as if the employer turned you down. But in reality, *you* rejected you!

In truth, many job descriptions get posted before a complete understanding of the organization's staffing requirements has been determined. They start interviewing candidates, and only then do they realize the specific elements of the role that are most critical to their needs.

Additionally, the employer isn't just looking for the candidate with the right combination of education, skills, and experience; they are looking for the person who will be a solid fit within their organizational culture. This culture fit or alignment is the element that often wins over everything else.

The two stories in this chapter may not seem typical. Rachel and Mari are extraordinary women. In their twenties, each dove into the world of work without college degrees and with only limited work experience. Then, they climbed up professional ladders that most people would only look at from the ground or a lower rung. Each, in their way, continued to put one foot ahead of the other—learning, growing and keeping an open, curious mind the whole way up. They made mistakes, learned from them, and forged ahead. Curiosity was and continues to be their primary driver, not their egos.

It may seem somebody afforded them special breaks that only a few can get, but before you draw any conclusions, take a closer look at their actions, decisions, and the spirit with which they traveled on their career paths.

Rachel Stewart

As a high school student, Rachel Stewart knew exactly what she wanted to do professionally. She was passionate about becoming an attorney. But Rachel felt she had a dilemma. She also really wanted to be a mother and could not envision how both could be done well simultaneously.

 I was trying to figure out how to find the balance between family and career. I wanted to be a mother, but I had a lot of ambition and didn't have many models for that. In 2000, I graduated high school and even then, I didn't see many women who were doing both successfully. So how I could pull that off? I'm one of those people who when I start something, I go all in. I knew it would be very difficult for me.

Rachel started college with some doubts about whether everything she aspired to would be possible. With law school in mind, she started in political science and quickly recognized that it wasn't the right avenue. Rachel considered nursing at that point, although she wasn't sure that was the right path either. Then she met her now-husband, Kent, who was working on his MBA, and they got married. She decided to leave school, figuring she would work to support him while completing his degree. Rachel planned to resume her education once she had clarified her goals. In the meantime, Rachel became pregnant with their first child, and over the next few years, their family grew. While she loved her family life and taking care of three young children, she was always learning new skills. Rachel started to do graphic design work and book layouts.

I did self-taught things and enjoyed creative work. We were plugging along, living the American dream, and bought our house in 2007 at its peak. Then 2008 hit; our home lost half its value overnight, my husband lost his job, and our third baby was just six weeks old. We were trying to figure out how we would make it all work and whether my husband was going to look for a new job—or if he was going to work for himself.

Kent opened an insurance agency, and they decided that Rachel would return to the workforce. It had been five years since she had worked outside the home. Around that time, Kent was contacted by a former business school classmate seeking an office manager/bookkeeper for his restoration company. "Well, for my money, I'd hire my wife," he said. "She does graphic design and accounting." Once Rachel spoke with the business owner, she clarified that she didn't have an accounting degree but had dabbled a little with QuickBooks. She believed that she was definitely unqualified.

The owner took a chance on me. I went through several interviews, and they saw potential in me. I was unqualified for the position on paper, but I was qualified to figure it out. I fell in love with the company, the integrity of the people there, and that we were doing something at critical points in people's lives. When they go through a flood, a fire, or something traumatic, we're meeting them on a terrible day. If we're doing our job right, we can help that process go better.

Initially, Rachel spent a lot of time figuring out how everything in the business fit together, what was or wasn't relevant, cleaning up the books, and getting processes in place. She read accounting books and watched videos online to learn everything she needed. For her, it was pure fun.

When Rachel began, the company had reached $1.5 million in revenue. The owner's goal was to increase revenues to $5 million over the next five years so that he could consider selling the company. Rachel was not planning to stick around that long, as she had intended the job to be a stopgap measure until Kent's business was stable. Then she would leave and find part-time work.

By 2010, only two years later, the company hit that $5 million mark. Rachel was still there full-time as she was fortunate to have family nearby who helped care for her children. The owner decided that he did not enjoy people management and decided to merge with another restoration company; but instead of one owner, there would be seven owners of this other company. The other company had even gone as far as to begin moving into their building, before the merger was finalized. Rachel approached her boss, questioning his decision to merge. She suggested that he hire a general manager who could deal with the people management, and run the company. Then, on the day he was supposed to sign the papers, her boss pulled out of the merger.

Two weeks later, Rachel was offered the general manager job. When she suggested that her boss hire a GM, she did not have herself in mind for the role. Rachel made it clear that she would be on a huge learning curve when it was offered to her.

She jumped into the opportunity with both feet and never looked back.

As the company was growing and scaling, they were running into issues with their job management software. The availability of what was out there to contractors was limited. Rachel was very frustrated. After doing the research, she decided that they needed to build the software. So they started a job management software company that was launched throughout the entire country for restoration contractors. It became a separate business that accelerated with several employees in place. Rachel became the CEO of that company while also running the restoration company.

 When I look back at it, there were some very low lows and very high highs, especially as I was trying to understand management practices. It felt like I was carrying the whole team on my shoulders, not because we didn't have talented people, but it was a product of my poor management. I have a lot of drive, and there were years when I wanted to bulldoze my way through the challenges. You must be comfortable with being unqualified and be willing to learn, grow, and self-evaluate.I was learning how to collaborate and how not to say, 'Come on, everybody; just follow me.' And then I'm looking behind and saying, 'Wait a minute, where is everybody?' I think it is really important to be able to recognize whatever is not working.

But that's not all, folks. Rachel started looking ahead with where they needed to take both the software company and the restoration company. She felt it was important to have a positive impact and reach beyond her day-to-day work inside the companies. Rachel decided to improve her public speaking skills and wanted to engage people on issues that she saw as common challenges for many. She also wanted to write a book.

Rachel hired a public speaking coach and started writing her book. She aimed to make this all happen quickly, because she was concerned about the perception that her speaking engagements and book writing might be misconstrued as distractions from her 'day job'. Yet Rachel needed to grow as a thought leader and influencer.

> The book and speaking engagements led to so much opportunity for the restoration business. I felt like being able to learn how to take ideas from inside my head and heart to come out in a way where I could convey passion, engagement, and invite people to move in the direction we were going…it really brought it all home together. It gave us exposure that we would have never gotten otherwise. So that which has helped our restoration business helps the software company. I thought it was a personal goal, but it influenced more than I would have expected.

Rachel was working on several big goals simultaneously. The development of the software was in beta, and she was launching a new company. Then she had some aggressive goals with the restoration company, as they were going to expand to the next level. Rachel was also releasing and promoting her book, *Unqualified Success, Bridging the Gap Between Where You Are Now and Where You Want to Be to Achieve Massive Success*[1]. She was feeling stretched—who wouldn't?

> Things that I was good at and confident about started slipping. For instance, I've always been a runner and have run ultra-marathons. At that

time, my younger brother asked me to be his pacer on a 100-mile run. It would be a commitment to train and run the last 20 miles with him. Normally that means you have nothing else going on. Let's not forget, I also have four children. Originally, I said no. Then I thought, this is going to be an experience that I would regret not being a part of. I called him back and said, Yes, I'll do it. I told myself this will be great, I'll be able to have a place to think and decompress, it will be therapy. In reality, I was so stretched that even the things I was good at were not the same. I had no passion around it and started having self-doubts thinking I'm failing on every avenue. Now I can look back and see it wasn't a failure, it was a capacity and focus issue. By the way, we did run together, and it was fantastic. I got myself together, made it to the finish line, and it was one of the most incredible experiences.

Once Rachel was able to step back and identify the issues that undermined her confidence, she could calibrate her capacity and focus so that when she felt stretched, she knew when to ease up. In mid-2020, Rachel left the restoration business to focus her efforts 100 percent on the software company, Xcelerate. Given how young the company was, she felt that she was heading into some unknown territory. Rachel knew it would have been safer to remain at an established company, but taking the risk to focus on Xcelerate full-time opened opportunities for her to become more fully involved in the business.

Today, Rachel shares her lessons learned with her children, encouraging them to be open to new discoveries, stretch their curiosity, and not let fear stop them from taking the next step.

Mari Ryan

Mari Ryan is the CEO and founder of Advancing Wellness, a workplace well-being firm that consults with organizations on creating people-centric cultures and practices. As an expert in worksite well-being, she has leveraged over thirty years of business experience in marketing, consulting, and executive roles across a variety of industries. Mari's mission is to create healthier businesses and positively impact the lives of employees through her consulting work.

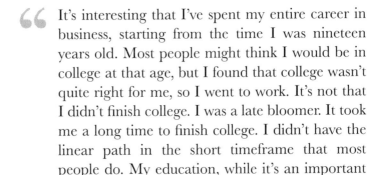

> It's interesting that I've spent my entire career in business, starting from the time I was nineteen years old. Most people might think I would be in college at that age, but I found that college wasn't quite right for me, so I went to work. It's not that I didn't finish college. I was a late bloomer. It took me a long time to finish college. I didn't have the linear path in the short timeframe that most people do. My education, while it's an important part of who I am, came later in life, after I had started to work in the business.

Mari has worked in a variety of industries and held different functional roles over the years—including sales, marketing, and operations management. She started working for a large insurance company in Hartford, Connecticut, that she really liked. Approximately every two years, Mari would make a lateral move to a role in a new department, staying at the same pay grade. Then within a year of that move, she would get promoted within that new job. As she describes it:

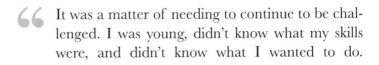

> It was a matter of needing to continue to be challenged. I was young, didn't know what my skills were, and didn't know what I wanted to do.

> Everything about it was exploration, learning new skills, and learning that, 'hey, I can do that too.'

The last of those moves was from a functional role into the corporate training department. Mari was twenty-seven years old and the only person in the department who didn't have a college degree. She had been assigned to work on a project that involved implementing new technology, which at the time involved personal computers. Mari didn't know whether she had any aptitude or skills for this, but someone in management had the confidence in her ability to work with the IT team and implement this new technology. Every day was a new challenge, and she was so eager to learn. Mari appreciated that they took a risk by giving her the opportunity to learn and grow on the job.

 I would say that one of my hallmarks—and this is a core principle which I think applies to anyone who is looking to expand their skill sets—is showing that eagerness to really learn. My drive and interest kept rewarding me in many ways with more challenging work and additional responsibilities over time, which was wonderful.

Mari left the insurance company for a position in the Boston area, where she had grown up. Once there, she decided to pursue her undergraduate degree. She was able to finish in a short period of time, because the college awarded her credits for life experience.

At that time, Mari made another big decision. She left her job, leveraging her experience in learning and development to work as a contract trainer—which landed her in very large corporate environments. Noticing that she was teaching many people who had MBA degrees, Mari found herself easily aligned with their skills and talents, even though she did not possess the same credential. Mari started to consider getting an MBA so that she could continue to learn, while increasing her earning potential. She also felt that she was underemployed in her trainer role and wanted to grow into something more fulfilling.

Mari attended Boston University's School of Management (my alma mater!) and found herself most interested in the marketing courses. By the time she finished her MBA, Mari was thirty-seven. She repeated her earlier strategy of starting at a lower-level in a new industry—high tech—and then getting promoted every couple of years to director-level marketing positions, eventually expanding those to include sales in her responsibilities.

 I kept growing and learning, being open to taking on new responsibilities, trying things I hadn't done before. Again, great managers saw that I was willing to step up and do what they asked me to do. I went from not knowing what I wanted in my twenties to training and becoming intentional in my thirties. I took a couple of other positions that were increasing in marketing responsibility; then I was laid off from one company in the early 2000s, just when the dot-com bust happened and the economy was tenuous. I started doing independent consulting and leveraging my skills and knowledge. I only had two clients over a two-year period, but I was consulting on a few different projects, and traveling 100 percent of the time.

Essentially, Mari was spending just one weekend a month at home in Boston. While she found the work interesting, Mari was acutely aware that she needed to do something different, as she felt her life was completely out of balance.

Mari hired a life coach, and they went through a series of processes—one which involved examining how she got her jobs. She found it to be meaningful, as they looked back to the first job Mari ever had as a day camp counselor when she was thirteen years old. They uncovered a pattern that Mari got her jobs through people who knew her, and she made that happen by meeting as many people as possible along the way. Sounds like she worked the magic of networking!

 I began to get focused, looking at health-related areas, but didn't have experience in the health field. So I went to a wellness conference and certification program. It was so interesting to be in the room with 90 people, many from clinical backgrounds, such as nurses and registered dietitians. Within a month of that program, I enrolled in a master's in health promotion program because I felt my MBA was an insufficient credential. It turns out it would've been fine. As I continued my education, the Massachusetts Department of Public Health invited me to deliver wellness services so I went from being a newbie in the field to serving as a subject matter expert. That relationship lasted for eight years, touching 120 Massachusetts employers and over 120,000 Massachusetts employees.

In 2006, Mari established her company, Advancing Wellness, which focuses on fostering healthy workplaces where employees can thrive. Mari and her team offer consulting, training, and speaking programs that bring workplace well-being strategies to support companies and their employees. Also, Mari wrote the award-winning book, *The Thriving Hive: How People-Centric Workplaces Ignite Engagement and Fuel Results*[2], a story about a CEO whose organization is no longer attracting nor retaining the employees required to remain competitive and keep their customers satisfied. The book is written as a parable set in two beehives—comparing each to an organization that can either support or diminish the well-being of its employees.

Mari is the co-founder and former chair of the board of directors of the Worksite Wellness Council of Massachusetts and is actively involved in the National Speakers Association New England Chapter.

Rachel's and Mari's experiences are distinctive in that they each started their careers in professional roles without the experience or education that would normally be required for their jobs. You could say they were *lucky*, since they were each given a big chance by the managers who hired them, knowing they had a lot to learn if they were going to be successful.

While they were certainly *in the right place at the right time*, there is research that makes the case for them being more than *just* lucky. Psychology Professor Richard Wiseman at the University of Hertfordshire in England has been studying luck for over two decades. In his book, *The Luck Factor: The Scientific Study of the Lucky Mind*[3], he identified four common attributes amongst people who are characterized as lucky. One, they are outgoing people who stay in touch with their networks throughout their lives. Two, they listen to their gut instincts and follow their intuition when making important decisions. Three, they are optimistic by nature and expect to be lucky. Four, while they experience all of life's ups and downs, they find the good in most circumstances and transform negative situations into something positive.

In addition to those four characteristics, Rachel and Mari demonstrated other qualities that contributed to their ability to learn and grow professionally. They were exceptionally open to trying new things, maintaining their eagerness to learn what was required to be successful on the job. Neither of them seemed to be hampered by insecurities or negative self-talk that would impede their progress. They did not hesitate to ask questions and freely engaged people across their networks when they needed information. Their outlook was consistently positive, supported by the habits of remaining curious, creative and always checking their assumptions before drawing conclusions or making decisions. As a result, both Rachel and Mari have emerged as leaders each in their respective industries.

We are all unqualified for that next step. If you want to stay in a place where you are qualified, you have to be content with no growth. Otherwise, you have to be comfortable with being unqualified and willing to grow.

—RACHEL STEWART, AUTHOR, *UNQUALIFIED SUCCESS: BRIDGING THE GAP FROM WHERE YOU ARE TODAY TO WHERE YOU WANT TO BE TO ACHIEVE MASSIVE SUCCESS*

Reflective Questions and Guiding Activities

Most of us have read a job description that captured our interest only to not apply because we believed we did not possess enough of the qualifications, and assumed the employer would not consider us a viable candidate. The truth is we are not mind readers and do not really know what the employer is seeking in a candidate and very often, the job description is written in general terms that do not capture the critical elements of what is needed to fill the role. So, we turn down the job before we have even given ourselves the chance to receive an offer.

Self-Assessment

On a scale of 1 (very uncomfortable) to 10 (completely comfortable), what is your general comfort level with attempting to do something new or unfamiliar to you? Think of something(s) you are genuinely interested in or intrigued by.

> What does your score mean to you? Be as specific as possible in articulating your feelings and thoughts about your experiences with trying to do something new.

> If your chosen score was two to three points higher than your original score, what would your experience look like in terms of your thoughts, feelings, and activities related to pursuing something new or unfamiliar?

> What kinds of information, relationships, or opportunities become available to you at this higher score?

What might get in the way or prevent you from elevating your score?

What actions, small, medium, or large, can you take to raise your score in the next three to six months? If you have difficulty thinking about your options, speak with a trusted colleague or friend to percolate a few ideas.

Here are some suggested activities that you can try to move your professional journey forward:

Try a Returnship

Return to work programs have grown rapidly to address the workforce needs of employers and adults ready to return to work after taking time away from regular employment. There are agencies that place people in returnship positions and many companies now have in-house programs. Some of these positions become full-time employment opportunities. Similar to internships, these programs provide people returning to work the chance to experience new careers and industries. See the Resources section for more information.

Community Colleges and Other Educational Options

Whether or not you have a four-year degree, you may want to learn a new skill or earn a professional certification. Community colleges specialize in serving adult learners who are preparing for the world of work and often provide cost effective options that serve a wide variety of needs. Your public library is a great place to start looking for information about your educational options. Librarians are highly skilled in uncovering information and identifying resources we were not aware was available. They also know how the material is organized saving you time and effort in locating helpful items.

UNCERTAINTY IS A FACT OF LIFE

It's not the events in your life that determine who you are,
it's how you choose to respond to them.

—Viktor Frankl

Life is full of uncertainty. While we know this to be true, it doesn't ease the pain when we are caught off guard by unexpected or difficult circumstances. We try to prepare ourselves for uncertainty and say philosophical things like, "Life is short. All we have is today. You never know what tomorrow will bring. "

Yet how often do we hear or say those phrases and let them float by, as we busily scurry around doing everyday things? We say, "One day I will…" or "When things settle down, we will…" I get uncomfortable when I hear someone talk about their job in disparaging ways, adding "I only have five more years until retirement. Then I'll be ___(fill in the blank)_." Then you'll be what? Five years older, for sure. What else?

Hey, look, I understand the bazillion practical reasons why people put things on hold or tolerate an unhappy work situation to meet responsibilities or longer-range goals. And I know just as many people who reflect upon their lives with a long list of regrets that they cannot change. It's not easy to be present or "live each day as if it is your last," making choices that put your well-being, happiness, and sense of meaning on the front burner. Yet there's tremendous value in planning with intention, and having a vision for your fulfillment.

So how can we be present in our daily lives and plan ahead with a sense of purpose and meaning?

At times, life has a way of putting that question squarely in front of us. The three stories shared in this chapter illustrate how and why people took different directions after experiencing unexpected, irreversible events that would change their lives forever. Think about what you would do in their shoes, or notice what goes through your mind as you read their stories. Take a few uncensored notes for your eyes only. Let your thoughts and feelings marinate for awhile to notice what else surfaces in your mind. Is there something you'd want to begin to plan on doing differently? You will notice that none of the three people profiled here made overnight changes even though their situations could have provoked dramatic actions.

Luis Velasquez

Luis Velasquez grew up in poverty in Guatemala, Central America, during the country's civil war. As a child, he knew no other reality.

 This is how we lived. I went to school and saw who disappeared, who died, or who was kidnapped that weekend. What are we having for dinner? No, ARE we going to have dinner? That was my normal. I didn't know any better. Yet I was a happy kid. Looking back, I don't remember being afraid, sad, or hungry. My parents were loving and supportive.

When the war ended, the United States in collaboration with Georgetown University set up Scholarships for Peace to offer a university education to young people from conflict-torn areas of the world. Students were given the opportunity to learn English and receive a liberal arts education so that they could return to their country and become beacons of change. Luis was awarded one of these scholarships. He learned English and earned an associate of science degree. It was the first time Luis understood that the conditions and circumstances of his childhood were "not normal." He also began to envision that if he worked hard, he could go far in the US. Luis then returned to Guatemala for three years to fulfill his commitment to the scholarship program, with the full intention of returning to the US to continue his education here.

During his third year back in Guatemala, Luis realized he couldn't afford to return to the US on his own, so he looked for scholarships and found one through the Department of Education in Florida. In order to qualify for the scholarship, he had to get accepted to a Florida-based school. Luis got into Florida A & M University and earned his bachelor's degree in agricultural science. While there, he had an assistantship with a professor who invited him to stay on to do a master's degree in his lab. As Luis completed his Master's, he was recruited by several PhD programs and ended up at Michigan State University in the Department of Botany and Plant Pathology.

Most of the work Luis did for his doctoral degree was in the lab of a world-renowned professor in the plant sciences. While the average PhD student would spend six years completing the requirements, Luis finished in four. When he came to the US, his dream was to return home and become a farmer. Luis's aspirations shifted, however; he decided he wanted to become a university professor.

Once he completed his PhD, Luis was hired immediately as a visiting assistant professor of fungal genetics at Michigan State University. He was well on his way to achieving his career goal.

Around that time, Luis got married. He and his wife built a house. He was on the path to a tenure track position that would enable him to realize his ultimate goal of becoming a full professor. Life was going extraordinarily well, given the odds for someone who grew up in poverty during a civil war.

Then, Luis was diagnosed with a brain tumor.

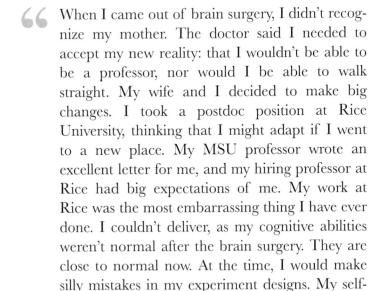

> When I came out of brain surgery, I didn't recognize my mother. The doctor said I needed to accept my new reality: that I wouldn't be able to be a professor, nor would I be able to walk straight. My wife and I decided to make big changes. I took a postdoc position at Rice University, thinking that I might adapt if I went to a new place. My MSU professor wrote an excellent letter for me, and my hiring professor at Rice had big expectations of me. My work at Rice was the most embarrassing thing I have ever done. I couldn't deliver, as my cognitive abilities weren't normal after the brain surgery. They are close to normal now. At the time, I would make silly mistakes in my experiment designs. My self-confidence was low. I survived the tumor, but neither my professional dreams nor my marriage did. My wife asked for a divorce. Imagine going to school for years, attaining your professional dream, then finding yourself lost and alone.

Luis had just one question for himself, "What are you

going to do about this?" He started thinking about what direction he would take and imagined the possibilities. First, he focused on getting his health back, so he started running. He ran his first marathon exactly a year after his brain surgery (after the doctor told him he wouldn't walk straight ever again!).

Professionally, Luis started to explore his options, staying open to a wide range of ideas. He considered all kinds of possibilities including real estate, car sales, Walmart greeter, and running a taco truck. He reflected on conversations he had with his wife about her work in human resources and thought about that as a possibility. Luis started to read about the field and decided to apply for human resource positions. Of course, he knew he wasn't qualified; he didn't have the experience or the degrees to back it up, but that did not stop him from trying.

Luis believes it only takes one person to believe in your potential to make strides, and in this case, he was right. A new friend gave him the opportunity that he needed. He took a job with a US-based consulting company whose niche was working with American companies in developing economies. Luis was hired as a consultant in Saudi Arabia. The caveat was that the Middle East was in the middle of a war, and Westerners were fleeing the area.

 The person who gave me that role took a big chance on me, and I am very grateful for that. Looking back, I realize that all the things that I've accomplished were a product of somebody believing in me. Somebody trusted me and saw my potential. So, I took that chance, and it actually worked out really well for me. This was the break I needed to reinvent myself.

And then, I was in my office at the company in Saudi Arabia, when the VP of HR came in and asked me if I could help him with a presentation. I went to his office and helped him with his presentation. I was coaching him without realizing it. That was the first interaction we had of many. He would ask so what about this...what about that...and we found a path forward together. One day, he asked me to help somebody else. The next thing I knew, I was traveling throughout the Middle East coaching executives. Eventually, I was moved from Saudi Arabia to Bahrain and did some work in Jordan, Kuwait, Egypt, Dubai, and Sub-Sahara Africa. I loved it.

After two years in the Middle East, Luis moved back to the US in 2007. He realized that he was on solid ground in human resources and consulting, but his educational background did not support the career trajectory he was on. So he went back to school and got an MBA in organizational leadership. He started traveling to Latin America (Brazil, Argentina, Mexico) in a new business development position.

Luis felt like he had reinvented himself. He loved what he was doing, and all was going right in his world. He also found love again. Luis married a kind, strong, and successful doctor, and he cemented his love of running. He became an ultrarunner.

 In 2012, I had just finished running the Western States 100-mile Endurance Run. I was in the best shape of my life. Then I went to see a new doctor for a regular brain check, and the MRI showed some terrible news. My brain tumor was back, yet I wasn't experiencing any symptoms at all. The doctor looked at the MRI before he saw me.

When he came in, he asked me, 'Where is the patient?'

I said, 'I am the patient.'

He said, 'That's not possible. The MRI I saw is of a person who I would expect is having major neurological problems; you seem normal. What have you been doing?'

I was somewhat surprised, and I responded, 'I've been running.'

'Well, whatever you're doing, keep doing it. It appears that your body is adapting to the tumor; perhaps it is because you are in a pretty good physical shape. But having said that, you have a ticking bomb in your head. We need to deal with it.'

So, I was like oh F**K, not again. I was picturing myself losing my job, getting divorced, and starting anew once again.

It went differently this time around. I got out of the hospital five days later and took some time off. My wife didn't leave, and I could still recognize my mother. However, my employer decided that they couldn't give me any more time off, and I was let go. After all, we were in the middle of a recession.

Luis still needed some recovery time before he could fully immerse himself in a job search once again. The economy was not doing well, and Luis encountered a tough job market. Then one day, he happened to be in a job interview, and the interviewer told him that they probably would not hire him because he "wouldn't be a fit for their culture." In an interesting twist, the interviewer told Luis that he was leaving the company, and he needed someone to help him transition out. Would Luis help him?

He became Luis's first coaching client, and instead of looking for more jobs, Luis started looking for more clients.

That was in 2013, and Luis has spent little time looking elsewhere. He has expanded his coaching practice to serve leaders in corporations such as Google, Twitter, SalesForce, Amazon, Genentech, and many others in the Silicon Valley of California. In addition, Luis facilitates a class called Interpersonal Dynamics at the Stanford University Graduate School of Business. He is a recognized expert on resilience, and he is committed to helping people to adapt and thrive—building resilience.

People have asked Luis over the years how he stays positive given that he has endured many traumatic setbacks and remains at risk for a recurrence of his brain tumor.

 To tell you the truth, I don't see this as an incredible feat. I simply focus on what I can control and let go of what I cannot control. I call them gravity problems and situational problems. A gravity problem is the tumor, which I cannot control. The fact that I lost my job was a gravity problem. However, I can control my response to those things. That is my situational response, so I ask myself, what am I going to do about it? What works for me is thinking about my desired outcome. I envision the possibilities and my first step to moving in that direction. Some people are suspicious that I look at things too positively. It doesn't work for everybody. Yet over time, I have learned that at the core of my transformation is resilience. I am a resilient individual. And to me, resilience is the ability to adapt to your circumstances. It takes three things: commitment, persistence, and optimism.

People might label Luis a survivor based on all he has been through in his life, but he has a distinct philosophy about his situation, as you would gather by now. He much prefers to identify as someone with resilience who has adapted to life's events as they occur. Luis believes that adapting is not the same as making changes. The distinction is significant in seeing how people approach problem-solving to improve things in their lives.

 Adapting is not changing. A difficult problem doesn't necessarily require a complex solution. You need to figure out the smallest adaptation that you can do with the lowest amount of effort. Those small adaptations lead to big changes over time. Those tiny adaptations have a cumulative effect. So instead of saying, 'I have to change,' try 'I have to adapt.' It's more palatable and easier to accomplish.

Luis's approach to his life and career is inspiring and demonstrates the true spirit of *resilience*—a word that gets thrown around a little too lightly, too often. Not only has he developed a thriving executive coaching practice, but he and his wife are also raising two beautiful children. He also continues to enjoy good health.

Michael O'Brien

When was your last bad day? For Michael O'Brien, it was July 11, 2001, the day he was struck head-on by a speeding SUV while out on a training bike ride. In many ways, Michael says his last bad day was one of his best, because it sparked his transformation from "human doing" to "human being." It changed his sense of purpose from leading sales and marketing strategy across his company (doing) to contributing in ways that did not compromise his values (being). He shares his journey in his memoir *Shift: Creating Better Tomorrows; Winning at Work and Life*[1]. He donates the book proceeds to World Bicycle Relief.

Michael describes himself as a kid who was more interested in sports than school or going along with society's linear notion of: graduate from high school, go to college, and get a job. His role models were his parents; Dad was in sales, and Mom was a nurse. Michael discovered his passion for sales and marketing in college, combined the two, and went into pharmaceutical sales after graduation. At the same time, he fell in love with a wonderful woman and married her. They had an awesome life together, and he started working his way up the corporate ladder.

> I didn't know anything about gratitude, mindfulness, meditation, vulnerability—all the things that are commonplace today. I knew none of that; I just kept going. Like a hamster on a wheel, I just kept on running. I was really good at putting conditions on my life—and not in a great way. I would often say to myself and others, 'I'll be happy when I get promoted,' or 'I'll be happy when I get to buy that fancy new car.' I would tell my wife, 'It's just busy right now. Once the meeting is over, it will be slower.' I was very much a human doer. That's how I lived my life until my last bad day.

Michael had a big company meeting in New Mexico. He flew out there from his home in New Jersey and brought his bike with him, as he had a goal to ride his bike in all fifty states. Michael was training for a big ride and especially enjoyed getting outside after sitting in a hotel conference room all day.

I thought I was being smart about bringing my bike as a good diversion. On the fourth lap of my little loop that morning, the SUV came swerving into my lane, at about forty miles an hour, hitting me head-on. I remember everything about that morning, from me hitting the grill into the windshield, the screech of his brakes, and the sound I made as I came off of his hood and onto the asphalt below. Then of course, one can imagine I became unconscious. When the EMTs arrived, I regained consciousness. I knew life was going to be different from that moment on. Just the thought of moving was painful. Anyone who is a cyclist can appreciate the question I asked the EMTs: 'Hey, how's my bike?'

It's remarkable how much Michael was aware of his experience of the accident and the subsequent events; many people do not have such specific recall. He shared that he consciously tried to stay alert, as he wanted a sense of control. At the time, Michael had a fear of flying, so when they brought in a helicopter to fly him to a trauma center, he asked if they had to go on, knowing it was non-negotiable. At that moment, he told himself, "If you live, Michael, life will be different. It has to be different. You have to stop chasing your happiness."

The doctors later told Michael's wife that had he been ten years older or not in good shape, he certainly would have passed away before he arrived at the hospital. The big thing that made it a life and death situation was his femoral artery in his left leg was lacerated as a result of his left femur having been shattered.

 It was an unbelievable pause button. Everything came to a screeching halt. It was really the start of awareness for me. I probably had some signs in my life that things were not necessarily as aligned as they could be. I was just busy on my hamster wheel, and I never saw them. This accident, my last bad day, stopped me dead in my tracks.

After four days, Michael came out of the ICU, and he started learning about the accident. The doctors painted a fairly grim picture of dependency and limitations along with more surgeries that would be required. He spent another week in New Mexico, and then was flown back home to New Jersey. Michael went to one hospital and then was admitted to the Kessler Institute for rehabilitation, where Christopher Reeve, our generation's Superman, had been when he was injured from his equestrian event. After a few months, Michael went home and continued with outpatient rehab for the next couple of years. He was concerned about being a big burden to his wife, because she was transporting him back and forth forty-five minutes each way. They also had two young daughters.

Michael started to pay attention to all the losses and the things he couldn't do anymore. He got a different picture of life; yet, he had made this bargain with himself that if he lived, life would be different. But would it be darker? That's the life that the doctors were painting.

 The doctors were trying to be kind. They didn't want to get my hopes up. It became like, oh my God, my life is over. Then I had a big moment of reflection...as I was in a rehab session, looking around at other patients and said to myself if you want a different life, Michael, you need a different frame. It was the first time I saw how I was showing up and being honest to say you're not giving it your all. Certainly, I had physical limitations, but my mindset was problematic because I wasn't giving it all that I could, in terms of my energy, and focus. That was big—like, hey, Michael, you can pay attention to what you're feeling and thinking. When you pay greater attention to these things, you can see you have choices. I don't have to be defined by this accident. I can be defined by how I respond to it.

Michael developed a three-pronged approach to supporting his recovery mindset: awareness, acceptance, and action. He believes in small steps, as they lead to much bigger gains. As already described, he developed his awareness and acceptance of his situation by reframing his mindset and expanding his choices. Part of his action was to develop a mindfulness practice and time to be quiet every day. In the evening before he goes to sleep, he incorporates a gratitude practice.

Michael also developed a mantra, "I'm gonna work really hard today to create a better tomorrow," which he then shortened to "creating better tomorrows"—where he was going to get one percent better every day. During his rehab sessions, his physical therapist would measure his degrees of flexibility and extension. Michael always wanted to move the needle one degree better every day, working on small steps with focus.

On October 10, 2001, Michael returned to work on a part-time basis, as he continued with his intensive rehabilitation. Not only wasn't it the same world he left, because he was changed, but the 9/11 attacks were a fresh and open wound for everyone around him, as his company was based in the metropolitan New York area. Questions and thoughts swirled through his mind as he re-entered this world that were in the background for months.

Michael wondered what "society" expected of him now that he had been through a near-death experience. Looking at role models who had been through comparable circumstances, he asked himself if he should follow their example in some way? Should he do a lot of speaking about "when bad things happen to people"? Maybe some travel to Nepal and go trekking, climb Everest, or do an iron man. These were questions that he struggled with for a while, as he returned to his regular life.

 Should I just quit my corporate job, and go find myself? Then, I thought I'm still the provider for my family. My wife and daughters are counting on me, I'm counting on me! I love what I do. I made the commitment to let go of the comparison. One of my favorite phrases is 'Don't compare your beginning to someone else's middle.' Let go of the comparison between what you have, what others have, and all that is the lens of scarcity or limitations. I also started giving up on big career goals. I was VP of North America sales and marketing for a top pharmaceutical company. I didn't set out for that. I decided to be true to my integrity, authentic to the situation, and do great work that would honor my values.

Before the accident, Michael's mindset and approach were clear: get a job, climb the corporate ladder, work toward the next level, and be happy there. He began to realize that as you go higher, you might lessen the degree to which you're doing it on your own terms because you have to play the game.

Michael decided that when he returned to work, he was not going to play the game. It didn't mean that he was immune from corporate politics, but he was determined to find approaches that didn't compromise his values. He made the commitment to stay as long as he could remain in line with his standards. In 2014, the company made some changes, and Michael realized he could no longer honor his values working there. It was time to leave. Michael already knew that he would be doing the work he does today, as the seed had been planted from his ICU bed shortly after his accident.

When Michael was in the ICU after his first surgery, he told his wife in a drug-induced state to: "Find David, follow David Kolb. He is our leader." David Kolb was the first executive coach he'd worked with as part of his corporate experience for many years. Michael found David's calm demeanor and zen-like approach to problem-solving, stress, and relationships to be a refreshing alternative to the people he interacted with day-to-day.

Michael liked this coaching thing, so when he left his corporate job, there was no doubt what path he would take next. He wanted to follow David Kolb's example and have the same positive impact on people's lives that he had experienced in his years working with David.

Initially, people who knew Michael were surprised by his choice to take the entrepreneurial route as an executive coach and consultant. They assumed he would join another pharmaceutical company—keeping his big salary, healthcare benefits, bonuses, company car, and international trips. Instead, Michael put up a website, and as he said, "I showed up on my terms."

 It looked like a pretty charmed life. For me, it was no, no, no, no.... This was about pursuing a purpose that had a whole bunch of passion in it. For me, this was easy. Yes, I had to go buy my own healthcare, the paycheck didn't come in every two weeks, and I had to figure out a lot of stuff. I was not on social media and didn't know any of that. All I knew was I wanted to help people change through sharing my story.

Michael shared his story, "My Last Bad Day," with clear and positive intentions. He has moved forward to recover, both physically and emotionally, well beyond the predictions originally given to him by his doctors.

Michael believes that all the events in our lives are neutral until we label them. As adults, we label things as good or bad, because we have contexts within which to make a judgment about them. He maintains that if we reframe those perceptions, we gain new meanings and approaches to things that could be far more productive. Michael made a conscious choice to hold a new mindset, energy, and work ethic in his life and career after his accident.

Does he have setbacks? Yes. Does he have strategies for dealing with them? Yes. Is life perfect? No, but he will be the first to tell you he is having a blast.

Michael will also tell you he wasn't alone. He had his peloton, and it has expanded in ways he could not have imagined.

> A peloton...is a group of cyclists in a bike race, and they're all working together. They need connection and trust to go down the road as safely and fast as possible. I'm here because of my peloton. One day in the hospital, I was thinking about all the people who were helping me—all the nurses. Of course, doctors are high-profile folks. My wife, my daughters, my friends, all the people behind my recovery. And I'm like, wow, they're my medical recovery peloton.

Today, Michael operates his executive coaching practice. He works with sales and marketing leaders, including managers/directors, c-suite, and entrepreneurs seeking to achieve success in their professional and personal lives. In addition, he offers the Pace Line Academy, a subscription-based professional/personal development program that includes one-on-one coaching, books that further growth, webinars, Q&A sessions, and self-paced courses. Michael speaks and writes regularly on a range of topics: resilience, change management, motivation, mindset, leadership, diversity and inclusion, and culture building. The media often seek him out for comments and interviews and corporations and groups for keynote speeches.

Michael delivered a compelling TEDx Talk, "We Go Where Our Eyes Go," about his near-death experience and the power of perspective. He shared the story about his cycling accident and how it sparked a journey where bad moments stopped turning into bad days. In addition to his first book, Michael wrote *My Last Bad Day SHIFT: How to Prevent Bad Moments from Turning into Bad Days*[2]. In March 2020, Michael launched *The Kintsugi Podcast*, a weekly show focused on conversations about resilience. He also posts a weekly video to his subscribers offering inspiring lessons, including the reminder to "PBR": *Pause, Breathe and Reflect™*. From the early days of his recovery to today, when Michael feels overwhelmed or life is moving too fast, he paused, took a breath, and reflected to help him be *mindful, present, and intentional*. It's a breathing technique that helps to slow things down.

Michael's pause, breathe and reflect practice has resonated widely. He created a design for T-shirts, mugs, and hats sold on his website. He also hosts multiple daily Pause, Breathe and Reflect meditations and discussion sessions on Clubhouse.

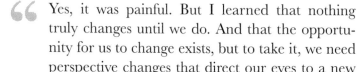 Yes, it was painful. But I learned that nothing truly changes until we do. And that the opportunity for us to change exists, but to take it, we need perspective changes that direct our eyes to a new place.

Jenny Lisk

Jenny Lisk is an author, speaker, and host of *The Widowed Parent Podcast*. Jenny never expected to be a widowed parent. Who would?

 We had two kids who were busy with school, scouts, and sports. I was involved as a Cub Scout and Girl Scout leader. Between kids and work, life was full. We had a dog, a cat, a house, a mortgage —and my husband, Dennis, and I both worked full-time. Then in May 2015, Dennis told me that he'd been feeling a little dizzy. It didn't seem like a big deal—maybe he was just a bit dehydrated, or wasn't getting enough sleep. Who knows? But very quickly, it was diagnosed as terminal brain cancer. There was no fixing it. It was glioblastoma, which is a very aggressive form of brain cancer. Beau Biden, John McCain, and Ted Kennedy all died from the same brain cancer. We went to see his primary care doctor—who sent us to a neurosurgeon the very next day. The following day, Dennis had his first brain surgery. He was sick for eight months and died here at home in January 2016. Our kids were nine and eleven years old at the time.

Jenny is passionate about helping widowed parents improve their family's well-being. Throughout Dennis's illness and after his death, she felt there was a gap in resources and guidance for parents in her situation. Two years after losing her husband, she left her corporate job and decided to do something about it.

From an early age, Jenny was drawn to doing something meaningful in the world, although she never would have imagined that one day she would become a champion for widowed parents and their grieving children. As a kid, she wanted to be Perry Mason, the fictitious criminal defense attorney who always took on seemingly indefensible cases. Jenny's mother had introduced her to the books, and she loved the TV show, which originated in 1957, long before Jenny was born. She was also inspired by her mother, who ran for and served two terms on the City Council in her hometown, Redmond, Washington. As a ten-year-old, Jenny was ringing doorbells, passing out brochures, and holding signs on election day— waving at people driving by to remind them to vote. She enjoyed these experiences and felt they deeply influenced her formative years.

Jenny majored in political science and economics in college, starting at Willamette University in Oregon. During the summer after her sophomore year, Jenny got an internship with her Seattle-area congressman, working in his DC office. The politics bug bit her. She just had to return there.

In the spring of her junior year, she transferred to George Washington University in Washington, DC. She secured another internship, this time with her senator's office, working eighteen hours a week.

In addition to her full course load, and the role in the senator's office, Jenny worked weekend nights at a George-town restaurant as a hostess to help cover her expenses. She was motivated and engaged in everything she was doing, determined to make the most of her time in the nation's capital.

After her junior year, Jenny decided that it would be fun to have a summer adventure and earn some money. She went to Alaska and spent the summer working in a fish cannery. The days were long, and the work was grueling, yet she gained a perspective there that she would not have gotten otherwise.

Working long hours, seven days a week—from 7:30 in the morning, until about midnight—I remember walking back to my room late one night and thinking wow, this is hard, exhausting work. Someday, when I have an office job, I should remember this hard work. No matter how hard a future job might be, sitting in an office and going to meetings will be cushy compared to standing fifteen to sixteen hours a day in rubber boots that hurt my feet and wearing a yellow rain suit covered with fish blood and guts. I should remember this experience, because it's going to serve me well someday. After this, I know I can do other things that are hard.

Little did Jenny know that two decades later how suddenly difficult her life would become.

As graduation approached, Jenny considered staying in Washington, DC, as she was interested in politics; however, she knew that entry-level political jobs would not pay well, and the cost of living was expensive. So she moved home to Seattle and got a policy job at the Seattle Chamber of Commerce. Jenny didn't like it as much as she thought she would, so she left the Chamber to pursue a project she had been pondering: writing a guidebook for interns in Washington, DC. She also enrolled in a bartending class to get her certificate so that she could earn an income while working on the book. The book project was short-lived, however, as Jenny found it was too challenging to engage from afar in the research and networking she needed to complete it.

It was the mid-nineties, and the internet was starting to take off. While Jenny was still working on the guidebook, she started creating a website. She realized that she could help people and companies by developing websites for them. Jenny went to Barnes & Noble, where they had a big computer section. She would sit there for hours, studying the web design books and deciding which one or two she would buy. Within a short time, Jenny had created a few websites for clients. In fact, her new business was a catalyst to how she met her husband.

Jenny became a delegate to the state political convention. Dennis worked with a think tank in Seattle that had a booth at the convention. Jenny was walking around, looking at the booths and wondering if she could create websites for any of these organizations. She stopped and talked to Dennis, giving him her card. The think tank called her; they had a meeting and hired her to build a website for them. In the process, Jenny got to know Dennis, and once the project was completed, they had their first date.

While she enjoyed the work, Jenny felt that her website business wasn't really going anywhere. She decided to attend graduate school to get an MBA with an emphasis on marketing and entrepreneurship. During her time at business school, she did an internship for a company that was using recycled tires and tennis shoes to create basketball floors that would play like wood but have a lower impact on joints. They offered her a job upon graduation, but she only worked for them for a short time as they ran out of funds.

Considering her options, Jenny looked toward the technology arena. Her sister was working for IBM in New York and offered to pass her resume around there. Within a few months, Jenny was hired for a role in New York. She and Dennis had married six months prior, and they saw this move as an exciting new chapter in their lives. Dennis enrolled in graduate school at NYU to study urban planning, and Jenny began her twenty-year affiliation with IBM.

After five years in the New York area, Dennis wanted to move back to the Pacific Northwest, because it offered great opportunities for urban planning professionals and would put them closer to their families. Jenny gave notice at her job, but they wanted her to remain and offered her the opportunity to continue working remotely. She thought it might just be a short-term solution, as she wasn't sure how it would work out.

Jenny and Dennis relocated to Portland, Oregon. Jenny continued to do project management and business analyst work at IBM. As a business analyst, she was the "middleman" between the business process experts and the technical experts, bringing them together to create and deploy new systems to support the leasing division of IBM's business.

 I learned a tremendous amount being in a large established company, working on complicated issues with highly experienced people. At some point, though, I began to feel as if I was just spending all my time helping IBM write more leases and make more money. One could look at it differently, but it felt that way to me. I wanted to do something more meaningful, but I was having trouble defining what that would look like. I was casting about for ideas, and it was complicated by the fact that I had a spouse who was in a lower-paying field. By then, we had two kids, a house, a dog, and responsibilities. I didn't feel like I could afford to pick something, spend ten years doing that, and then have it be the wrong choice for me. I didn't want to make a change unless I was pretty sure that it would be a good move.

At one point, Jenny thought seriously about going to nursing school. She looked at the prerequisites and how to get into the programs, discovering that she didn't have some of the prerequisites. So Jenny enrolled in a Psychology 101 course at Portland Community College, which would have been a prerequisite for nursing school. She thought it would be a fun, interesting experiment to take one class at the community college.

Jenny enjoyed being back in school but found that the demand of doing homework, along with a full-time job and family life, was difficult to manage. They had just adopted their second child, so they had a baby and a toddler at home. Simultaneously, the economy was beginning to suffer due to the impending financial crisis of 2008. Dennis was anticipating a layoff from his job, and he was seeking a new role in Portland—or Seattle, where they both had family.

In 2008, Dennis landed a role with the planning department for the City of Redmond, Washington, in the greater Seattle area. Jenny continued her remote work for IBM while continuing to ponder more meaningful options.

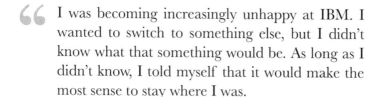

> I was becoming increasingly unhappy at IBM. I wanted to switch to something else, but I didn't know what that something would be. As long as I didn't know, I told myself that it would make the most sense to stay where I was.

From the time they moved to Seattle until 2015 when Dennis got sick, life was full for Jenny's young family. She had a busy full-time job, and Dennis worked full-time for the city. From the moment he told Jenny he felt dizzy, it was only a few weeks until Dennis was diagnosed with glioblastoma, an aggressive form of brain cancer. Cognitively, he was never the same after his first surgery. Jenny's life, as a wife and mother, was changed forever.

> My managers at IBM were incredibly kind and accommodating. I was Dennis's main caregiver, a demanding role, and eight months is a long time to juggle caregiving with work. In the first few months, I only worked a tiny bit, and for the last

several months, I worked part-time on a flexible schedule, as there were unexpected needs that would pop up, such as trips to the hospital. I really appreciate that my managers made it work. Dennis's office was also wonderfully supportive. They sent cards, visited frequently and participated in a program where employees could donate leave to Dennis, enabling him to receive his full salary. Because of their generosity, he never had to go on disability, which would have been a reduced salary.

Throughout Dennis's illness, Jenny kept in touch with people by writing updates in a CaringBridge journal. Caring-Bridge.org was established in 1997 to enable families going through a health-related crisis to communicate with family, friends, and colleagues in one centralized place. People could subscribe to Jenny's CaringBridge journal and receive notifications when she posted an update. They could send messages of support and offers of help to her there.

Dennis passed away eight months later in January 2016. He was forty-four years old.

 I went back to work about three weeks after Dennis passed away. I felt like we had eight months of all this trauma. Now it seemed like things would be back to 'normal,' but obviously, they weren't. I had a CaringBridge journal when he was sick, and many people were following along, including my colleagues. I think that was helpful, because a situation like this can be awkward. I wrote a post, I think the title was 'Kicking the Elephant out of the Room.' In it, I said, 'I'm coming back to work next week, and the kids are going back to school, so let me just kick the elephant out of the room. Here's what's going on with us. If you see me, it's OK to say something.'

Jenny continued to work for **IBM** but also considered what else she might want to do. She started to see a therapist and found their discussions to be helpful, not only about her grief but about life. Jenny took the time to reflect on her whole experience of illness, cancer, death, and grief. She noted gaps; in particular, the widowed parenting part of her journey proved to be the most difficult. There were plenty of resources for *adults* experiencing grief. She had a great therapist and read a lot of books, but Jenny wasn't finding many resources for *parents whose kids were grieving*. She believed she could step in and try to help fill the gap.

 I spent more time casting about. What should I do? Did I need to become a therapist, or get some type of additional credential or degree? Did I have the time or money to go back to school? It still wasn't clear what the steps would be, but I started talking to people, asking questions, and thinking about how to approach the problem of the lack of information and resources for widowed parents. I got the idea that I could start a podcast.

Still at **IBM** as a certified project manager, Jenny was required to renew her credential every three years by earning professional development certification hours. She was listening to every project management podcast that she could find just to get the hours, regardless of the topics or speakers.

One of the project management podcasts that Jenny stumbled upon was an interview with strategy consultant and executive coach Dorie Clark. Dorie was launching her second book, *Stand Out: How to Find Your Breakthrough Idea and Build a Following Around It*[3]. Jenny read the book and took voracious notes, something she had never done before when reading a book. She talked to her therapist about the book—and about starting a podcast for widowed parents.

 I realized I could explore this topic with a podcast by interviewing people who had something to say about different pieces of this puzzle. Whether people who had written books about grief, anxiety, children's grief, or other widowed parents who had been down this path, I could talk with them about their reflections and experiences. It could be adults who lost a parent when they were young, reflecting on what they wished people had known or done, what helped, and what didn't. A podcast is a way to gather information and connect with someone who I wouldn't ordinarily get to speak with. I realized that if I was struggling with this and seeing this gap, there were likely other widowed parents with the same questions and struggles—and a podcast could be a helpful resource for them.

When Jenny had originally started thinking about alternative career options years earlier, she had read a book about taking a sabbatical called, *Reboot Your Life: Energize Your Career and Life by Taking a Break*[4]. Jenny found it appealing but didn't know how she could make a sabbatical work. She read the book twice more over the next few years, and by the third time, she was considering starting the podcast.

Around the same time, IBM switched their strategy on employees working remotely and decided to consolidate their workforce into different offices. Jenny was informed that her job was being moved to New York, and the company offered her a relocation package.

 My kids were just starting middle school and high school. Why would I move for a job that I'd been thinking of leaving for years? And why would I move for a job that I might get laid off from? So, these things all came together. I was reading Dorie Clark's stuff and thinking about rebooting with a sabbatical. It all came together. I decided I wasn't moving for IBM. I would declare a one-year sabbatical. I would start this podcast and see what I could do in this widowed parenting space.

Jenny launched the *Widowed Parent Podcast* in November 2018, shortly after she left IBM. She gave herself a year to build up an audience, get involved in the parenting and grief fields, and meet people. Since then, Jenny has interviewed experts, authors, widowed parents, and grieving children. She has reached people globally with her podcast.

Two years later, Jenny wrote and released her memoir, *Future Widow: Losing My Husband, Saving My Family, and Finding My Voice*[5].

 When Dennis was sick for eight months, I was writing consistently in the CaringBridge journal, sharing openly with people who cared about what was happening. People seemed to appreciate it and a number of them commented that I was a good writer. It seemed like this body of writing could be a helpful glimpse into behind the scenes of what's going on in a family where one of the parents, who are forty-something with two young kids, is terminally ill. Eventually, it came into view, and I was ready to turn this into a memoir.

It seemed like it fit nicely with what I'd been doing with the podcast, and would hopefully be helpful to my listeners and others.

Over the course of her sabbatical, Jenny has been connecting with grief centers and related organizations across the US and Canada to communicate her message about the need for specific support for widowed parents. In addition to interviewing many of these people for her podcast, Jenny has developed relationships with many experts and researchers who have published studies and books about parenting and childhood grief. They have supported her podcast and her memoir by reviewing her manuscript and writing endorsements for the book.

 When push came to shove, I had to get really honest with myself:

Would I work to support my comfortable lifestyle, or would I work to make the world a better place for widowed parents—even if it meant potentially compromising that lifestyle?

Once I got clarity on the question, it became easier to see the answer.

You see, Dennis died—*but I didn't.* Living as he did to age forty-four, he got something like half a life. If I live the rest of my life half-heartedly, it would almost be doubly tragic.

And I felt like that is what I had been doing—and would continue to do, if I didn't make a significant change.

So, now, I had to choose what was next for me. And…I *got* to choose.

Somewhere in my post-loss obsessive reading binge, I stumbled across the idea that one should imagine life in five years, and ask themselves this question: *if my life is the same five years from now as it is today, would I be OK with that?* If the answer is no—or especially if the answer is *hell no*—then *now* is the time to do something about it.

I told the world I was taking a one-year sabbatical to see what I could do in the area of widowed parenting. I figured I could always go find another tech job in a year if it didn't work out.

I was pretty sure I wouldn't be exercising that escape hatch.

Excerpted with permission from *Future Widow: Losing My Husband, Saving My Family, and Finding My Voice,* by Jenny Lisk

In addition to supporting widowed parents and their children, Jenny has written articles and created how-to videos to inform "grief allies"—the people who want to help those who have experienced a loss. Some of her videos and articles include, "Twenty-five Practical Ways to Help a Friend through the Illness or Death of a Spouse," and "How to Write a Condolence Card."

At the end of her one year sabbatical Jenny realized that she wasn't finished with this work. She continued writing and podcasting while single parenting two teenagers. Jenny is planning to write books for kids who've lost a parent and a handbook for widowed parents. She also speaks at conferences, grief centers, and community groups. Jenny plans to continue to put her grief into action and service.

You may wonder why Michael's, Luis's, and Jenny's stories are included here in a book about breaking through the obstacles to define a career that fulfills you. Naturally, their journeys were intertwined with the devastating events in their lives. Yet they emerged from those experiences in ways that opened them up to career choices they likely would not have considered before. Of course, I wish they could have gotten there in less traumatic ways.

Greatness comes by beginning something
that doesn't end with you.

—Robin Sharma

Reflective Questions and Guiding Activities

We know that life can change in an instant. Thinking about the fragile nature of life serves to remind us to both appreciate every moment, and to not get complacent about our goals. We also need to give ourselves space to live at a pace that enables us to blend a sense of being present in the moment while planning for and looking forward to the future.

Self-Assessment

Think about a typical or random weekday in your life. This can be a snapshot in time, choose whatever comes to your mind in this moment. On a scale of 1–10, how would you rate it? There is no right or wrong number.

1 = Most days are nothing special; they run into each other.
10 = Every day feels precious; I never take a moment for granted.

> Based on the rating you gave, what does that day look/feel like to you? Describe it briefly.

> Are you OK with the rating you chose? Why or why not?

> If you are not OK with your rating, what would you like it to be, regularly? What would those days look like?

> Now that you have read this book, what stories or examples have resonated most with you? Why? Is there one step you are prepared to take to increase your

sense of fulfillment, meaning, and satisfaction in your work. What will you do?

Who will you share your progress with and possibly ask for support? What other resources might you need to go forward?

Imagine it is one year from now. What has changed in how you feel about your work and/or life as a result of making this change?

CONCLUSION

IT'S TIME TO ACT

Remember you are half water. If you can't go through an obstacle, go around it. Water does.

—Margaret Atwood

As I write this, it is day 332 of the pandemic. Some of the international borders are closed. Everywhere we go, people are wearing masks. On a daily basis, the media broadcasts the number of new positive cases reported and COVID-related deaths. Talk about *uncertainty*! *Unprecedented times*!

Those phrases have been spoken ad nauseam, and while they convey a truth, I believe they give people permission to feel powerless. No doubt, this has been an extraordinarily challenging time, and for some, that may sound like an understatement. But COVID-19 is not the first period of uncertainty we've experienced—nor will it be the last. As you read this, you may be living in a very different time from when I wrote the book; yet change is a constant.

As we learned from the stories of Luis, Michael, and Jenny

in Chapter Nine, life can change in a moment; it is *always* uncertain. We can only be prepared just so much. One of the core principles from my initial coaching training that provided the most valuable foundation for me professionally and personally is this: our clients are *creative, resourceful, and whole.* It took me a while to get this in my bones, but once I did, it changed the way I handled every relationship in my life, not just with my clients. It definitely helped me to be a better parent!

Imagine if we saw ourselves and others as creative, resourceful, and whole when we encountered any goal, challenge, adventure, or unexpected event in our lives. What becomes possible? Stop for a moment and think about it.

Certainly, no one anticipated we would still be here with the pandemic. Throughout this time, I have been fierce in my resolve to stay healthy, positive, and supportive of everyone whose path I crossed. Now, don't get me wrong. I've had my dark moments. I am deeply distraught by how divided our country has become and heartbroken over the widespread, tragic loss of lives that has occurred. But I have taken that disturbed energy and turned it into proactive efforts, mostly writing this book and broadcasting new episodes of my weekly podcast, *Work from the Inside Out.* I also renewed my practice of offering talks for job seekers, sponsored by local libraries— something I had reduced in recent years, as I began to focus on work beyond my geographic area.

Working from home was not new for me, yet sharing space 24/7 with my husband and grown daughter (for six months) added many nuances that required adjustments, aka first-world problems. It has also offered conveniences that enabled me to "work smarter", in many cases. I could move from one meeting or activity to another smoothly and feel a sense of accomplishment in ways I had not experienced before.

So, while I was doing much of the same work I had been enjoying for many years, I felt a more profound sense of purpose in it, especially in coaching clients who were daunted by the uncertainty of the economy. Adding the development of my creative self as an author offered a bright silver lining to what could have been a much darker time.

Across the globe, people's lives have been changed in dramatic ways. For some, they have experienced devastating losses and traumas they may never recover from. Others will move on and regain some semblance of life as they knew it before. Perhaps they will even be able to put this all behind them and not look back.

As of this writing, I know many people who are making vows to go forward, committing to taking less for granted, and making their choices count even more. I do wonder how many will stay on track, or will it just be like another New Year's resolution? All too often it goes like this: By February or March, they stop going to the gym or say, "I can take care of this another time." Weeks turn into months, and months turn into a year. Then what? Another year has passed, and little progress has ocurred.

Do not allow that to happen!

I hope that the stories told here inspired a more profound journey to clarify your priorities and gain a clearer sense of direction to take purposeful action. This process can take some time. Be patient with it and yourself. Let the stories sit with you, and notice what surfaces in your mind as you reflect on their journeys and lessons learned.

You may be reading this at a time when life has opened up again; you are no longer required to wear a mask at the grocery store and can attend a gathering of more than ten people. You can be with your loved ones, friends, and coworkers regularly now. Your life is back to "normal." Yet, how have you been changed? What did you discover about yourself during and after the pandemic? What assumptions or expectations did you have about how life would be once most people were vaccinated? How were your career and work-life affected by the experience? What are you doing differently now? Or what would you like to be doing differently now?

If you are reading this well after the COVID-19 crisis has been stabilized, have other significant changes occurred that impacted your life? How has time or history provided perspective on the pandemic and its changes? Are you where you want to be now? Or are you headed in the direction you want to be going?

If you have not already begun to do so, I am asking you, here and now, to take the incremental steps you need to make meaningful changes that will bring more satisfaction and fulfillment into your life. Not only do you have twenty-two stories laid out in front of you, but you also have your reflections and answers to the questions and exercises at the end of each chapter.

To help you get started, I offer you the following guidelines to ground you as you go forward:

Do not do this alone! As I have said before, no one is truly successful in a vacuum. Two heads are better than one; possibly more than two is best! Developing this book, I had the steady guidance of a wonderful writing coach as I created my first draft, and weekly meetings with my book accountability buddy who was also writing a book. Mari Ryan hired a coach when she left the insurance business and moved into the wellness sphere. Rachel Rice was engaged in the world of mindfulness and energy medicine long before she departed her corporate job. The list goes on and on. When I say do not do this alone, I recommend that, in addition to people, you access other types of resources such as professional associations, courses, books, articles, websites, etc. I've included a resource section at the end of this book to help you get started in that direction. I also suggest using your public library, as reference librarians are an often-overlooked resource who can help to pinpoint all kinds of information. They want to help, and their services are generally free.

Network, network, network. Aka connect, connect, connect, and when you think you have exhausted everyone you know, believe me, you haven't. While it doesn't require you to "kiss every baby and shake every hand," you want to stay open to expanding your sphere of connections. It is not just about what you are getting out of it, but also about what you can give. Dorie Clark and Mac Prichard volunteered on political campaigns, resulting in strategic contacts that became solid, long-term relationships—helping them make connections to the next steps in their careers and beyond. Giving is where the secret sauce is. As I've shared, Dale Carnegie said, "To be interesting, be interested." Serve on a nonprofit board of directors, or volunteer for a special project with your favorite organization. You'll develop new relationships—while having the opportunity to potentially collaborate with others whom you didn't previously know—and add new experiences to your resume. Most people find their next opportunity through a connection, and you never know when that contact may turn to you for a favor. Networking is a two-way street. As you go about your day-to-day life and meet people, intentionally or otherwise, remember to ask them if they would recommend anyone else you should speak with. That next person you meet may be where the magic is.

Be open to possibilities. When I hear someone say, "I was just lucky," it sounds as if they played no part in making something good happen. Even lottery winners had to buy the ticket! Lucky people are generally walking through life with their eyes open and their hands stretched out, ready to receive something good. When Luis Valesquez was at his lowest point, he had a friend who gave him a chance even when his qualifications didn't fit the job. Why? His friend knew he would give it his best effort, because by nature, Luis has an extraordinarily positive work ethic. Mari Ryan was given the chance to work on a project implementing new technology even though she did not have the qualifications, because she had demonstrated her eagerness and ability to assimilate new concepts and skills quickly. This experience became the catalyst for her to pursue a college degree.

Believe yourself to be a "lucky" person. What does this mean? We learned about Rachel Stewart's and Mari Ryan's journeys and how they initially progressed in their careers without the experiential and educational backgrounds normally required. Stanford Professor Dr. Carol Dweck, author of *Mindset: The New Psychology of Success*[1], has done extensive research on people's beliefs in their most basic talents and abilities. She distinguishes these beliefs into two mindsets: fixed and growth. Fixed mindsets are characteristic of people who believe their abilities, traits, personalities, and talents are set, they are unchangeable. People in a growth mindset seek constructive criticism, and ask for feedback from others because they want to improve and believe that's how their talent will develop. Obviously, a growth mindset is the recommended strategy here. It also creates opportunities for mentoring, resulting in people investing in your growth, thus setting the stage for luck and good fortune to show up. As you can see, however, luck doesn't always just appear like magic, as we imagine it does. We can create the conditions to attract it, beginning with believing in our talents and ability to learn.

Catch yourself when your mind spirals into a sea of obstacles. Many of us have had repetitive thoughts run through our minds for years, such as: *I'm not good at…, I'm too…, I can't…, They won't…, I'm not enough of…, I shouldn't….* You know what I mean. These thoughts are sneaky, because they run through our subconscious minds in a way that we may not notice. Yet they can influence our self-esteem, beliefs, and behaviors—holding us back from our best selves. Petra Kolber's story offered us a great example of how she was always aiming for perfection, and it took a toll on her mental and physical health. It takes practice to put that negative self-talk aside and walk around it, so you can see where you want to go while believing you can get there. There are many great resources to help you with this (see Resources section). My wish for you is to go from the *have-to's* to the *want-to's* more naturally than ever before in your life. Practice … practice … practice …

Listen to your gut. Rachel Stewart's story is a great example of someone who trusted her gut instincts. In her early years at the restoration company, she had little experience or education to launch from in making decisions and navigating her role. She leveraged her natural talents, confidence, and instincts to establish herself as a leader. Jay Vogt trusted his values, which were his gut, so to speak, and they have guided him successfully through his primary consulting practice and a few other side businesses. Too often, we allow our logical minds to cloud our intuitive thinking, and this is when we tend to move in a less satisfying direction. It may work to meet certain needs—such as financial obligations or to meet other people's expectations—but ultimately, we are left feeling like something is missing or more. My recommendation is to listen carefully to your intuition, notice what your logical mind is trying to do, and find a meaningful place to take action. You do not need to make an all-or-nothing move in one direction or the other. A conversation with a trusted ally or a coach can be beneficial in discerning what thoughts are inviting opportunity—and what is keeping you in a holding pattern that doesn't fulfill you.

In closing, engage with people, make use of the resources available to you, and most of all, get out of your own way! Define your path to a more fulfilling life, and it will not only be better for you, but it will serve everyone around you. The Resources section will help you get started. Wishing you curiosity and fulfillment as you carve your path forward toward greater purpose and meaning in your life.

Die with memories, not dreams.

—Andra Watkins

A NOTE FROM TAMMY

Thank you for taking the time to read *Work from the Inside Out*.

One last thought before you place the book on the shelf and return to life as you know it.

I urge you to ask yourself, as Jenny Lisk asked herself:

 If your life is the same five years from now as it is today, would you be OK with that? If the answer is no—or *especially* if the answer is hell no—then *now* is the time to do something about it.

Well … what are you waiting for?

Sending my best wishes to you,
Tammy

RESOURCES

Recommended Books

<u>Career Strategy</u>

Bill Burnett & Dave Evans, *Designing Your Work Life: How to Thrive and Change and Find Happiness—and a New Freedom—at Work* (Vintage, 2021)

Dorie Clark, *Reinventing You: Define Your Brand, Imagine Your Future* (Harvard Business Review Press, 2017)

Dawn Graham, Ph.D. *Switchers: How Smart Professionals Change Careers and Seize Success* (AMACOM, 2018)

Mark A. Herschberg, *The Career Toolkit: Essential Skills for Success That No One Taught You* (Cognosco Media LLC, 2021)

B. Jeffrey Madoff, *Creative Careers: Making a Living with Your Ideas* (Hachette Go, 2020)

John Neral, *Your Mid-Career GPS: Four Steps to Figuring Out What's Next* (LLH Publishing, 2021)

Susan Peppercorn, *Ditch Your Inner Critic at Work: Evidence-Based Strategies to Thrive in Your Career* (Positive Workplace Partners, 2018)

Michael Bungay Stanier, *Do More Great Work* (Workman Publishing Company, 2010)

Workbooks

Bill Burnett & Dave Evans, The *Designing Your Life Workbook, A Framework for Building a Life You Can Thrive In* (Clarkson Potter, 2018)

Jane Horan, Ed.D., *Now It's Clear, The Career You Own* (Springtime Books, 2018)

Fran Hauser, *Embrace the Work, Love Your Career: A Guided Workbook for Realizing Your Career Goals with Clarity, Intention, and Confidence* (The Collective Book Studio, 2022)

Shift your mindset

Richard Carson, *Taming Your Gremlin* (Quill, 2003)

Dorie Clark, *The Long Game: How to be a long-term thinker in a short-term world* (Harvard Business Review Press, 2021)

Dr. Carol Dweck, *Mindset: The New Psychology of Success* (Ballantine Books, 2007)

Leslie Ehm, *Swagger: Unleash Everything You Are and Become Everything You Want* (Page Two, 2021)

Laura Gassner Otting, *Limitless: How to Ignore Everybody, Carve your Own Path and Live Your Best Life* (Ideapress Publishing, 2019)

Networking

Morra Aarons-Mele, *Hiding in the Bathroom: How to Get Out There When You'd Rather Stay Home* (Dey Street Books, 2017)

Dale Carnegie, *How to Win Friends and Influence People* (Simon & Schuster, 2010)

Keith Ferrazzi, *Never Eat Alone, Expanded and Updated: And Other Secrets to Success, One Relationship at a Time* (Currency, 2014)

Rebecca Otis Leder, *Knock, How to Open Doors and Build Career Relationships That Matter* (An Inc. Original, 2021)

Jayne Mattson: *You, You, Me, You: The Art of Talking to People, Networking and Building Relationships* (Jayne Mattson, 2019)

Robbie Samuels, *Croissants vs. Bagels: Strategic, Effective and Inclusive Networking at Conferences* (Movement Publishing, 2017)

Websites for job search and career exploration

The following websites are some of my favorite career and job search resources. They provide current, reliable information you need to keep your momentum going during a career discovery or transition process.

Resume Worded
https://resumeworded.com/

Resume Worded is an AI-powered platform instantly gives you tailored feedback on your resume and LinkedIn profile.

LinkedIn
https://www.linkedin.com/

LinkedIn is the number one resource for professional networking and visibility. Create your profile, join groups, connect with other professionals and expand your network, share information, and samples of your work. Learn about employers, company cultures, search job postings and apply for positions.

Job-Hunt
https://www.job-hunt.org/

Job-Hunt.org offers comprehensive, current job search and career advice from experts across the employment marketplace. This is your go-to source for the latest strategies on conducting an effective search to land your next role.

The Muse
https://www.themuse.com/

The Muse is a go-to destination for the next-gen workforce to research companies and careers.

Indeed
https://www.indeed.com/

Indeed offers free access to search for jobs, post resumes, and research companies.

Meetup
https://www.meetup.com/

Search Meetup.com to meet people, make friends, find support, grow a business, and explore mutual interests. You can find groups that share information on the job search or an industry marketplace, company leads, and professional development opportunities.

Pro tip: Seek industry-specific and professional association websites to locate resources for professional credentialing, training programs, courses, networking opportunities, and job postings.

Hire a coach

International Coaching Federation
https://coachingfederation.org/find-a-coach

The International Coaching Federation has a comprehensive listing of professional coaches that you can search by the criteria of interest to you.

The Muse career coaching
https://www.themuse.com/coaching

Muse coaches are broken down into three price levels: Mentor, Coach, and Master Coach. All of their coaches have been vetted and are backed by the Muse, and they each offer something different.

Free and low-cost online education resources

Many universities offer free or low-cost online courses taught by professors, providing learning opportunities for anyone seeking to expand their knowledge and reach in the job market. I have seen clients use these resources to learn new technical skills, for example, which enabled them to enhance their resume and increase their eligibility for certain jobs.

edX
https://www.edx.org/

edX offers high quality online courses from over 160 institutions who share a commitment to excellence in teaching and learning. They have everything from single free courses to certifications to paid degree granting programs at all levels.

LinkedIn Learning
https://learning.linkedin.com/

LinkedIn Learning offers thousands of professional courses that build in-demand skills needed in today's businesses and workplaces. To access the platform, you need to have a paid LinkedIn account although there are some free courses available.

Coursera
https://www.coursera.org/

Coursera provides flexible, affordable, job-relevant courses and programs from over 200 higher education institutions. They offer a range of learning opportunities—from hands-on projects and courses to job-ready certificates and degree programs.

Open Culture
https://www.openculture.com/

Open Culture brings together high-quality cultural & educational media for the worldwide lifelong learning community from top universities. Their offerings include close to 2,000 on-line courses from top universities, over 4,000 movies, 1,000 free audio books, 800 e-books and learning lessons for forty-six languages.

Planning for college and financing higher education

American Student Assistance (ASA)
https://www.asa.org/about-us/

American Student Assistance (ASA) is a private nonprofit that has helped students with college access and financing for higher education since 1965. With a mission to help students make informed choices to achieve their education and career goals, ASA is building on their expertise to impact students on a broader scale by engaging them as early as the middle school years. ASA offers a wide range of digital resources and programs that are worth taking the time to explore, especially if you are concerned about the cost benefits of investing in higher education and making the most of an education.

Consumer Financial Protection Bureau (CFPB)
www.consumerfinance.gov/consumer-tools/student-loans/

The Consumer Financial Protection Bureau (CFPB) is a federal agency that offers comprehensive information to the public on various financial matters. In plain language, they provide thorough explanations of financial situations making many programs and processes easier to understand and navigate. All resources are provided for free in multiple languages.

Podcasts

Podcasts are a great resource for job seekers and career changers. The shows included here are some of my favorites. Podcasts are an excellent way to gain knowledge and insights from top career professionals.

Work from the Inside Out podcast
https://www.tammygoolerloeb.com/podcast

Find Your Dream Job podcast
https://www.macslist.org/podcasts

Going Solo
https://smashingtheplateau.com/goingsolo/

Reframe & Reset Your Career
https://harshaboralessa.podbean.com/

Macs List 100 Top Career Podcasts List
https://www.macslist.org/podcasts/career-happiness/meet-the-top-career-podcasts-of-2021

I have been honored for the past three years to have my podcast included on the Macs List 100 Top Career Podcasts List. It includes over 100 career podcasts that may be related to your career goals.

WHAT YOU CAN DO NOW

Bonus: Work from the Inside Out companion workbook

As a special gift for you, I have created a companion work-book to enable you to work through with the questions and activities at the end of each chapter. There are bonus check-lists and additional prompts to help you think through your answers to the questions so that you can get the most out of this book.

You can access the workbook through this link:
https://www.tammygoolerloeb.com/workbook

Do a good deed and pay it forward

When we do a good deed for someone else, we are often left feeling better about ourselves. Wouldn't you agree?

You can perform a great deed and help a fellow reader right now. Go to this book's page on Amazon.com, and give it an honest rating and review. Consider mentioning a tip or idea you found useful. The goal of this book is to help as many people as possible find their way to more meaningful and satisfying careers, and reader reviews are a great way to make this happen.

Another way you can help others who are seeking to move their career in a new direction, is to post a selfie with the book on social media. In your post, share a helpful tip or two that you discovered while reading the book. Remember to smile!

Your actions will be paying it forward to others who are seeking more meaning and fulfillment in their careers. Doesn't that feel good? In advance, thank you!

Share with a friend

Do you have a friend who is ready for a career change? How about buying them a copy of this book and buddy up to work through the questions and exercises together? It is more effective to make changes when you have an accountability partner and the perspective of a trusted person with whom to bounce ideas around.

WORK WITH TAMMY

If you're interested in pursuing more meaningful and fulfilling career options, Tammy can help. Here are some ways she can support your goals.

Coaching

Coaching is a goal-oriented, collaborative process in which Tammy supports her clients to develop the clarity, focus, and structure they need to move their career plans forward. Whether you are seeking your next role, aiming for reinvention, or developing your executive presence, Tammy has the skills and tools to guide you in your best direction. She will partner with you to build a custom process that is designed to create your desired outcomes.

Small Group Coaching Mastermind Programs

Tammy has designed a program that blends the best of small group coaching with traditional peer mastermind formats. Starting with a curated group of four to eight professionals, Tammy develops a curriculum of content, structure, and coaching. She blends those elements into a program that leverages the wisdom and experience of the group's members to create opportunities for peer support and relationship building. While Tammy convenes and facilitates each group, essential ownership for the growth and outcomes rest within the group and individuals themselves as this is where the special sauce of group experiences are created. Three- and six-month programs with extensions are available on a scheduled basis.

Speaking

Invite Tammy to speak for your group, company, meeting, or conference. She will deliver a memorable speech and presentation that will inspire, educate, and entertain your audience. Tammy's personable, warm style translates across groups of all sizes. She engages audiences in an interactive manner, enabling their involvement with the content. Tammy speaks about career growth and fulfillment, workplace communication, leadership presence, and job search strategies.

Team Development and Training

One of the most important factors affecting employee engagement are workplace relationships. Tammy coaches leaders and teams to improve their communication skills, operations, and leadership development. She also offers interactive workshops on topics such as communication across the organization, managing upward, listening skills, coaching skills for managers, and difficult conversations. Tammy can plan your team's or organization's off-site retreat and provide facilitation for your group.

Find out more at tammygoolerloeb.com

NOTES

Introduction

1. Malcolm Gladwell, *Blink: The Power of Thinking Without Thinking*, (Back Bay Books, 2007)
2. https://www.gallup.com/workplace/352949/employee-engagement-holds-steady-first-half-2021.aspx
3. Richard Carson, Taming Your Gremlin: A Surprisingly Simple Method for Getting Out of Your Own Way (William Morrow Paperbacks, 2008)

1. Fear: Friend or Foe?

1. Richard N. Bolles and Katharine Brooks, *What Color is Your Parachute? Your Guide to a Lifetime of Meaningful Work and Career Success* (Ten Speed Press, 2021)
2. Petra Kolber, *The Perfection Detox, Tame Your Inner Critic, Live Bravely, and Unleash Your Joy* (Da Capo Lifelong Books, 2018)
3. Richard Carson, *Taming Your Gremlin: A Surprisingly Simple Method for Getting Out of Your Own Way* (William Morrow Paperbacks, 2008)

2. It's Never Too Late

1. Dorie Clark, *Reinventing You: Define Your Brand, Imagine Your Future* (Harvard Business Review Press, 2017)
2. Herminia Ibarra, *Working Identity: Unconventional Strategies for Reinventing Your Career* (Harvard Business School Press, 2004)

3. Too Many Responsibilities

1. Seth Godin, *Purple Cow, Transform Your Business by Being Remarkable, (Penguin Books, 2007)*
2. Dorie Clark, *Reinventing You: Define Your Brand, Imagine Your Future* (Harvard Business Review Press, 2017)

6. Success Is Not a Destination

1. Ron Carucci, Eric Hansen, *Rising to Power: The Journey of Exceptional Executives* (Greenleaf Book Group Press, 2014)

7. You Need to Network, but Not Just for a Job

1. https://www.merriam-webster.com/
2. https://www.louadlergroup.com/4-insights-that-will-enhance-your-passive-candidate-recruiting-efforts/
3. Robbie Samuels, *Croissants vs. Bagels: Strategic, Effective and Inclusive Networking at Conferences* (Movement Publishing, 2017)
4. Dorie Clark, *Stand Out: How to Find Your Breakthrough Idea and Build a Following Around It* (Portfolio, 2015)
5. Michelle Tillis Lederman, *The Connectors Advantage: 7 Mindsets to Grow Your Influence and Impact* (Page Two, 2019)
6. Dorie Clark, *Reinventing You: Define Your Brand, Imagine Your Future* (Harvard Business Review Press, 2017)
7. Dorie Clark, *Stand Out: How to Find Your Breakthrough Idea and Build A Following Around It* (Portfolio, 2015)
8. Dorie Clark. *Entrepreneurial You: Monetize Your Expertise, Create Multiple Income Streams, and Thrive* (Harvard Business Review Press, 2017)
9. Dorie Clark, *The Long Game: How to Be a Long-Term Thinker in a Short-Term World* (Harvard Business Review Press, 2021)

8. I'm Not Qualified. Do I Belong Here?

1. Rachel Stewart, *Unqualified Success: Bridging the Gap From Where You Are Today to Where You Want to Be to Achieve Massive Success* (Rachel Stewart, 2019)
2. Mari Ryan, *The Thriving Hive: How People-Centric Workplaces Ignite Engagement and Fuel Results* (Pequossette Press, 2018)
3. Richard Wiseman, *The Luck Factor: The Scientific Study of the Lucky Mind* (Arrow Books Ltd, 2004)

9. Uncertainty Is a Fact of Life

1. Michael O'Brien, *Shift: Creating Better Tomorrows; Winning at Work and Life* (Red Hill Pub, 2017)
2. Michael O'Brien, *My Last Bad Day SHIFT: How to Prevent Bad Moments from Turning into Bad Days,* (Peloton Coaching and Consulting, 2019)
3. Dorie Clark, *Stand Out: How to Find Your Breakthrough Idea and Build a Following Around It (Harvard Business School Press, 2017)*
4. Catherine Allen, Nancy Bearg, Rita Foley, Jaye Smith, *Reboot Your Life: Energize Your Career and Life by Taking a Break* (Beaufort Books, 2011)

5. Jenny Lisk, *Future Widow: Losing My Husband, Saving My Family, and Finding My Voice* (Bluhen Books, 2021)

Conclusion

1. Dr. Carol Dweck, *Mindset: The New Psychology of Success* (Ballantine Books, 2007)

ACKNOWLEDGMENTS

To Bob and Emma, my number one cheering section: you are my heart and my foundation.

To Peg Wallis, my "budster," your unconditional readiness to support and advise me on anything I am working on is deeply valued. I cherish you.

To Jenny Lisk, my book accountability buddy, publishing mentor, podcast twin, and dear friend: thank you for the countless hours exploring every inch of this process. We learned so much together, and had a blast doing it!

To Dorie Clark, and the Recognized Expert community: my deepest gratitude for your collective wisdom, generosity of spirit, and intellect. You are the gift that keeps on giving.

To Gen Georget, my writing coach: no matter how distracted or stuck I was, you were there offering prompts to unlock my creativity and find my voice. Heartfelt thanks to you and the Round Table Companies family for your vision and support.

To the fascinating people profiled in this book: Chip Massey, Petra Kolber, Sally Wovsaniker (as told by her son Alan), Arza Goldstein, Mark Dyck, Stacey Altherr, David Shriner-Cahn, Mac Prichard, Ron Carucci, Alisa Barcan, Jay Vogt, Rachel Rice, Corey Blake, Robbie Samuels, Dorie Clark, Rachel

Stewart, Mari Ryan, Luis Velasquez, Michael O'Brien, and Jenny Lisk. Thank you for generously sharing your stories. I know your journeys will serve to inspire readers to break through the obstacles that hold them back from pursuing work that is satisfying, fulfilling, and meaningful.

Special thanks to the following people for their support and encouragement: John Baldoni, Harsha Boralessa, Todd Cherches, Dorie Clark, Diana Wu David, Jennifer Fondrevay, David Gooler, Dawn Graham, Christina Guthier, Mark Herschberg, Malini Jayaganesh, Arlene Kapilow, Michael Leckie, B. Jeff Madoff, Ellen Meyers, Andy Molinsky, Laura Gassner Otting, Mac Prichard, Werner Puchert, SD Shanti, Ofer Sharone, Michael Bungay Stanier, Anne Sugar, Jacqueline Wales, Gina Warner, Alan Wovsaniker, Fei Wu and the Creative Entrepreneurs Mastermind, and Summer Zifko.

ABOUT THE AUTHOR

Tammy Gooler Loeb, MBA, CPCC, is a career and executive coach who helps people pursue meaningful and fulfilling work. In addition to coaching individuals, Tammy consults and speaks on career satisfaction, leadership development, effective workplace communication, and networking strategies. Tammy has enjoyed working with clients and companies across many industries for over two decades.

Tammy also hosts a weekly podcast, *Work from the Inside Out*, where she shares the inspiring stories and informative lessons of people who made professional transitions to more satisfying and fulfilling work.

Her expertise has been featured in *Harvard Business Review Ascend*, *Forbes*, *Fast Company*, and *The Boston Globe*.

Connect with her at tammygoolerloeb.com.

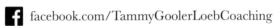 facebook.com/TammyGoolerLoebCoaching
twitter.com/tammygoolerloeb
instagram.com/tammygoolerloeb
linkedin.com/in/tammygoolerloeb

Made in the USA
Middletown, DE
03 January 2023

20784922R00149